GEMMA PETHERBRIDGE

Find *Your* Light

AWAKEN YOUR SOUL POWER AND EMBRACE YOUR CALLING

GODSFIELD

First published in Great Britain in 2026
by Godsfield Press, an imprint of
Octopus Publishing Group Ltd
Carmelite House
50 Victoria Embankment
London EC4Y 0DZ
www.octopusbooks.co.uk

An Hachette UK Company
www.hachette.co.uk

The authorized representative in the EEA is Hachette Ireland, 8 Castlecourt Centre, Dublin 15, D15 XTP3, Ireland (email: info@hbgi.ie)

Distributed in the US by Hachette Book Group, 1290 Avenue of the Americas, 4th and 5th Floors, New York, NY 10104

Distributed in Canada by Canadian Manda Group, 664 Annette St, Toronto, Ontario, Canada M6S 2C8

ISBN 978-1-84181-666-1
eISBN: 978-1-84181-667-8

A CIP catalogue record for this book is available from the British Library.

Printed and bound in China.

10 9 8 7 6 5 4 3 2 1

PICTURE CREDITS

Dreamstime.com: Mehmet Gokhan Bayhan 189 (15); Gemma Petherbridge: 189 (14); Holly Booth: 72, 78, 189 (1), 189 (10), 189 (12), 190 (4), 190 (5), 190 (6), 190 (13), 190 (17); iStock: Arisa Thepbanchornchai 117, Belmachia Othmane 43, benedek 190 (7), BruceBlock 114ac, 188 (5), bsiro 115, Candice Hamilton 189 (4), CAPToro 20, Diana Kovach 9, 18, 28, 30, 40, 44, 53, 54, 70, 84, 88, 98, 106, 118, 128, 142, 152, 162, 176, EyeEm Mobile GmbH 94, 186, fatido 124, Galeanu Mihai 131, 146, Helin Loik-Tomson 168, lefym Turkin 26, 35, 41, 64, 69, 105, 121, 140, 160, jakkapan21 63, 93, JKristoffersson 114br, johncopland 57, JustineG 171, Kerrick 188 (8), 189 (2), 190 (14), koyu 173, KrimKate 114ar, 114al, 188 (9), 189 (17), 189 (11), loveshiba 101, ma_rish 12, 32, 81, 85, 159, 163, 167, Mara Fribus 189 (3), Mariia Kokorina 114bl, MariuszBlach 154, mictian 10, nanako75 77, Nastya22 188 (4), nastya81 188 (12), peshkov 31, photodeedooo 189 (8), PICTEORICO 42, 49, 50, Ramziya Abdrakhmanova 110, RHJ 189 (16), saemilee 59, SageElyse 190 (16), seamartini 45, 180, sparkusdesign 90, Stellar-Serbia 190 (1), tenten 13, Tijana87 108, ttsz 100, Velishchuk 138, volgariver 4, VvoeVale 114, Walaiporn Sangkeaw 135, wiiz 188 (13), yotrak 14; Michelle Szpak: 132, 188 (7), 189 (5), 189 (7), 190 (11); Octopus Publishing Group: 188 (6); Michael Illas 188 (1), 188 (2), 188 (3), 188 (10), 188 (11), 188 (14), 188 (15), 189 (6), 189 (9), 189 (18), 190 (2), 190 (3), 190 (9), 190 (10), 190 (15); Sarah Ann Wright Photography: 114bc, 189 (13); Shutterstock: lushcool 16, 38, 82, 126, 182, SarraMagdalina 37a, Sophie Cyzewski 190 (12), vvoe 190 (8); Unsplash: Adam Ling 37, Jeremy Thomas 66.

STAFF CREDITS

Commissioning Editor: Louisa Johnson
Art Director: Jaz Bahra
Senior Editor: Leanne Bryan
Designer: Megan van Staden
Copyeditor: Matthew Cory
Picture Research Manager: Jennifer Veall
Assistant Production Manager: Lisa Pinnell

DISCLAIMER

No medical claims are made for crystals or essential oils in this book and information given is not intended to act as a substitute for medical treatment. Healing means bringing mind, body and spirit back into balance, it does not imply a cure.

SOURCING CRYSTALS RESPONSIBLY

Remember that crystals are a gift from Mother Earth, so please respect her and source your crystals responsibly. Ethical sourcing means educating yourself about where your crystals have come from, how they have been mined and the supply chain they have come through. The more we ask these questions, the more the crystal industry will realize how important these factors are to their customers.

SOURCING ESSENTIAL OILS

When sourcing essential oils, take care to ensure they are pure, non-adulterated and free from fillers and synthetics.

Contents

AUTHOR BIOGRAPHY

Gemma Petherbridge has always had one foot in the esoteric world. Growing up amid the mystical landscapes of Stonehenge and Avebury, she discovered she was psychic from a young age. But it wasn't until the loss of both her parents in her early twenties that her dreams of a corporate career gave way to a deeper calling – a need to explore life's bigger questions. Now, two decades on, Gemma is an international speaker on energy healing, holding over 27 qualifications across a wide range of spiritually therapeutic modalities. She is the founder of the award-winning Crystal Mystery School, an online academy offering live, accredited training in disciplines such as Crystal Healing, Akashic Records Reading and Cacao Facilitator Training. Having transitioned from healer to teacher, she has now taught and inspired thousands of people worldwide.

www.thecrystalmysteryschool.com
www.instagram.com/crystalmysteryschool
www.instagram.com/gemmapetherbridge

This is for my students, who have entrusted me to teach them the ways of the Lightworker. The joy I see this work gives you lights me up – thank you.

And to my Soul Family, particularly my mother and father, who taught me to live with purpose, and my husband, who always shares the path alongside me.

Introduction

Welcome, Lightworker!

Your soul came here with a mission, and this book will help you remember what it is.

If you have picked up this book, you are likely standing at a crossroads. You might be reflecting on your life, wondering which direction to take next. Somewhere deep inside, you sent out a silent call for guidance – and in answer this book has found its way to you.

Many people reach this moment in their lives; when questions, self-doubt and a quiet ache for something more creeps in. Perhaps your life so far has been shaped by pressure to achieve the milestones that society promises will bring happiness: good grades, the right career, the ideal partner, a home, a family. While these things can certainly be fulfilling, I have met countless people who have achieved them all, only to discover an emptiness they can't explain. Outwardly, it looks like they've 'made it', but inwardly it feels like something essential is missing.

Or perhaps those milestones have always remained just out of reach – not from a lack of effort or desire, but because life has placed obstacle after obstacle in your way. Maybe the journey so far has felt like a string of disappointments. On the surface, these two paths seem different, but they share one truth: the way we were told to live and the things we were told to want often fail to bring the deeper sense of fulfilment our souls are longing for.

This ache you feel – this urgency or pull to discover what's missing is a sign. It is a sign that you are awakening. This is just the spark that marks the beginning of a beautiful new journey. You've been guided here. Life may have sent you subtle nudges at first, gentle ripples suggesting you were meant for something else. If we ignore those whispers, they grow louder, becoming waves that shake us awake. This is the Universe insisting on change.

The good news is that once you begin to listen to this feeling, it can alter everything. One day, you will look back and see that *this* was the moment you began to step into a truer version of yourself, one that feels aligned, authentic and whole.

You have realized that you are here to walk a different path – one that might not yet be truly defined. Those parts of you that feel different, extra sensitive, or unconventional? They're not flaws; they're clues. Markers pointing you toward your purpose.

You are not alone in this. There are more souls on the planet right now than ever before. That is not a coincidence. One reason for this great gathering is to help humanity wake up. Like you, many people are starting to sense that their lives – even if successful on the surface – are missing something deeper. Their souls are calling to them. Something ancient is stirring. They're remembering who they are. And so are you.

You are a *Lightworker*.

> *'Your soul knows how to wake up, it's done it hundreds of times before.*
>
> *It chose this life for you so it could embrace that experience again!'*
>
> – THE AKASHIC RECORDS

What is a Lightworker?

A Lightworker is someone who uplifts their own life, and the lives of others, by living in alignment with their natural gifts. These gifts support, inspire and elevate rather than drain or diminish. When a Lightworker shares their light – just by being their authentic selves – they not only brighten their own path, but also spark others to step into their truth, creating real change, healing and transformation.

Lightworkers are wise souls who intuitively understand that empathy, compassion, community and inclusivity are not just nice ideals, they are the foundations of a meaningful and fulfilling life. Living in this way brings them joy because it allows them to naturally operate at a higher vibration.

Lightworkers are often drawn to work in environments or communities where the energy feels heavier or more challenging. They do this not because it matches their own vibration but because they feel called to bring light into those spaces and help uplift the collective energy. At the same time, they are also drawn to experiences, people and environments that keep their own frequency high, because deep down, they know they are here to follow what makes them feel truly alive.

If we were sitting together in a circle, and I asked you to close your eyes and quietly ask yourself, *Am I a Lightworker?,* many of you would feel a quiet but certain *yes* bubble up inside.

SIGNS YOU ARE A LIGHTWORKER

- You may notice that, more than most people, you appreciate stillness, find happiness in nature or feel wonder when gazing at the stars.
- Since childhood, you may have sensed that you were different. As you grew older, those differences became more apparent.
- You are slow to anger and tend to act from a place of love and empathy.
- Others may tell you that you have a 'healing presence' and that they feel lighter or uplifted after spending time with you.
- You are naturally drawn to self-development and spiritual books. Even if friends playfully call you 'woo-woo', you recognize the real value of the insights they contain.

Why Lightworkers are Important

The planet is lucky to have you.

Humans are at a turning point. Every day global news highlights destruction, division and pain, with people and governments driven by fear and personal gain – everything a Lightworker is not. The planet is under strain, and many systems are beginning to falter. The fearful energy is heavy and contagious, but Lightworkers are here to help shift this.

This book will show you how your energy can be a catalyst for change. Your commitment to seeking inner joy will naturally inspire others to do the same. When enough people begin living from joy, we will collectively move away from fear and into energies of love, compassion and empathy. You don't have to change the world, but as Gandhi reputedly said, you can '*be the change you wish to see in the world*'.

This book will guide you to live more fully, unapologetically and joyfully. My hope is that *Find Your Light* will help you remember who you are, reclaim your gifts and shine so brightly that your light becomes a beacon for those still finding their way.

MY STORY

Hello, from one Lightworker to another. I have been where you are now.

I've been psychic for as long as I can remember. For a short time, films like *The Craft* and *Practical Magic* made me feel a little more 'normal', but deep down, I always felt different, as though I perceived the world differently. I enjoyed school and had many friends, but other children often told me *'I was too nice'*, a comment that left me puzzled.

I remember my first crossroads moment. I was in the second year at university in the UK when both of my beloved parents passed away unexpectedly, just nine months apart. In the midst of grief and the dramatic life shifts this brought, all the expectations of who I thought I should be fell away. Up until that point, I had been a people pleaser, following my parents' hopes for me as closely as I could. Without them, far more possibilities opened up before me, and the idea of pursuing a coveted corporate job in the City no longer felt like my true path.

At the same time, a close family friend Lalli, who I think of as my surrogate grandmother, handed me a copy of Louise Hay's *You Can Heal Your Life*. Only a few pages in and I knew those insights would forever change how I saw the world.

Today, I run the Crystal Mystery School, an award-winning online international school that qualifies Lightworkers in holistic modalities and skills designed to empower them to support and heal both themselves and others. Every day, I witness people light up as they discover new abilities and achieve what they once believed impossible.

Seeing their joy fuels mine, and that's how I know teaching is my Soul Purpose and my Lightworker gift. The very qualities that once made me feel different are the same traits that now make me perfectly suited to my calling. I feel deeply fortunate that my work brings me joy every single day.

This book is a collection of the lessons I have learned along the way. The path has been far from linear – some of my choices were misguided. My hope is that, through my years of study and exploration, you can fast-track your journey and follow your calling more quickly.

If you feel alone right now, know that you no longer have to be. I will be your guide as you move through these pages. As you do the work and step fully onto your path, your energy will shift and you'll begin to notice your tribe finding their way to you.

Being a Lightworker is a gift, and I'm excited to show you why!

How to Use This Book

Find Your Light is a complete guide to the Lightworker journey. Together, we will explore what it truly means to be a Lightworker, look at the roots of your gifts and explore why you feel called to this moment in time. I will walk beside you as you discover your unique path, offering tools, practices and wisdom to step onto it with confidence.

We will move through a powerful process of healing: clearing old wounds, letting go of limitations and restoring balance to your energy body so you are no longer held back by past emotions, thoughts or behavioural patterns.

I will help you strengthen your intuition and introduce ways to connect with your spirit team. With this strong foundation of healing, you will be ready to accept your purpose, bringing your dreams into reality and walk your new path with clarity and authenticity.

To get the most from this book, I recommend reading it in order, since each chapter builds on the last, both in knowledge and practice. Some sections include journal prompts, so keep a notebook and pen close by to capture your reflections and insights. When we explore energy tools, you can work with the suggested essential oils and crystals, or simply choose ones that resonate most with you.

A Note on the Activations

At the end of each chapter, you'll find a suggested Activation: usually a visualization or short ritual. Think of an Activation as a modern form of initiation. Across cultures, initiations and rites of passage have long been used to mark key moments of transition and change in someone's life.

In this book, Activations serve as catalysts for growth, and memories from past lives can leave lasting imprints on our energy and even on our DNA. Each Activation is designed to help you rebuild energetic connections and unlock lost skills and insights. To receive the most benefit, try to complete each one as you reach it.

Preparation is important. Choose a space where you won't be disturbed and treat the experience as something meaningful. You might light a candle, play soft music, bring in crystals or diffuse essential oils – anything that helps you relax. A calmer mind and body will maximize the effects of each Activation. Learn that this is where you do this work, enabling you to relax deeper and maximize the effects of each Activation.

Other helpful tips are:

- Keep drinking water so you stay hydrated.
- Have your journal and pen ready to capture insights.
- Begin by closing your eyes, relaxing your body and gradually lengthening your breath. Once you feel settled and calm, move into the steps provided.

At its heart, *Find Your Light* is a guide for Lightworkers who are ready to embrace their full potential. What that looks like will be different for everyone since every soul is unique – especially that of a Lightworker. This book offers a wide tool kit of techniques so you can find what fits you best. Follow your joy, take what resonates and release the rest.

If you're ready, we can begin. It's time to walk the Lightworker path together.

THE AKASHIC RECORDS

Throughout this book, I will draw on the wisdoms of the Akashic Records – each chapter opens with a message from this realm. The Akashic Records are often described as holding the energies or frequencies of everything. Many envision them as a vast, energetic library where Intuitives and Channels can connect to gain insights into a soul's plan (more on that later). You can think of the Records as the energy of universal consciousness; a collective memory that holds information and wisdom about the past, present and future, and about why everything is as it is.

PART 1

Awakening to Your Light

'Enter this chapter as if I were about to tell a story; one you have both told and also played a role in yourself many times. Something new can also be something forgotten, and when you remember, your life will blossom.'

– THE AKASHIC RECORDS

CHAPTER 1

Lightworkers and the Awakening World

'I see you, and I ask you to remember. This wisdom will feel new and yet familiar. Honour those subtle feelings because they open doors.'

– THE AKASHIC RECORDS

Everything is Energy

You are both human being and a soul. Even though our bodies appear solid, our bodies are in fact made up of atoms, and each atom is composed of tiny particles (protons, neutrons and electrons) that are in constant motion, held together by electric and magnetic fields. This movement is not random; it's vibration, which is a form of energy.

So, while we may appear to be physical beings, at our core we are energy in motion. That energy has a frequency and both science and spirituality agree that these frequencies can be measured. Every thought you have, every emotion you feel and every belief you hold carries a frequency. Your cells are in constant dialogue with this inner world, shifting and adjusting in response.

When your higher awareness starts to develop – when you begin to feel greater love, peace or spiritual connection – your entire being vibrates at a higher frequency.

Your Soul Has a Story

Your soul is pure energy. The laws of physics tell us that energy can neither be created nor destroyed. This suggests that the soul's journey does not simply end with the physical body, but continues in another, through a process some traditions call 'reincarnation'. Each soul, including yours, has lived many lifetimes.

To understand Lightwork, we need to understand the soul's purpose. To understand the soul's purpose, we must also consider the soul's history.

It is important to note that many Lightworkers feel they are not originally from Earth. Some identify as Starseeds – souls believed to have lived cycles on other planets or star systems. We will explore this further in Chapter 2. Whether Starseed or not, all Lightworkers share a deep longing to live with purpose, to remember why they came here and to help raise the collective vibration.

Earth is a Mystery School

In Ancient Egypt, there were Mystery Schools that offered spiritual lessons to Initiates, who had to master each stage before progressing to the next. Planet Earth itself functions as a Mystery School for Lightworkers who choose to incarnate here in this lifetime. While Earth is not the only 'school' a soul can attend, it is considered the most advanced; souls aspire to experience a physical body and life in the third dimension. This allows them to engage with:

- TIME: In other Mystery Schools events can unfold instantly. However, on Earth there is a need to give situations time to unfold so souls can learn to trust and appreciate the cycles and seasons.
- POLARITY: This allows us to experience contrasts such as light and dark, love and fear. It will bring an understanding of balance and cultivates empathy and the need to see a situation from different points of view.
- FREE WILL: Once a soul reincarnates it is free to make its own choices and react to Earth's experiences in any way it wants.
- PHYSICAL PLEASURE: As an energy being, life on Earth allows our soul to experience the physical form. The aim is full embodiment, embracing the pleasure and sensations our physical body offers.
- DIVERSITY: Earth is rich in different people and experiences, giving souls a lesson in understanding and appreciating different cultures, different ways of thinking and different ways of being.

The physical nature of Earth enables us to learn lessons much faster than in other realms. Life here acts like a spiritual accelerator, because it presents challenges including:

- Hardship
- Contrast (polarity)
- Choice (free will)

Earth encourages growth through experiences like love, relationships, illness, loss, survival and responsibility. We are regularly confronted with situations that evoke strong emotions, triggering soul lessons, such as:

- Forgiveness
- Compassion
- Boundaries
- Trust
- Surrender
- Courage

By comparison, these lessons can take a much longer time to learn in higher dimensions or more peaceful, non-physical planets, where there is generally less friction.

WHO CREATED IT ALL?

Who or what created our souls is a complex question. To shed light on it, I turned to the Akashic Records (see page 15), which offered this explanation:

> *'It does not need to be so closely defined as one name; that will distort its essence. It is everything. We come from it, and we are it. When you can love everything, you will gain a deeper understanding of what it is.'*

For the sake of this book, I will use the term 'the Universe' to describe this powerful source as it feels as inclusive as the Records suggest.

Why We Have to Forget

Just as we aren't allowed to take our course notes into an exam, when our souls incarnate on Earth, we lose conscious memory of the goals we intended to achieve so that we can reach them authentically. To make us forget, veils are added to our energy fields, allowing us to fully inhabit the physical body and egoic mind without constant interference from higher awareness.

It is possible to remove these veils. Individuals who experience spiritual awakening often describe it as a lifting of the veils, which enables a deeper sense of connection with their soul, its gifts and the Universe (see page 21). Now, we will explore how memory and awareness begin to return as the veil starts to lift.

ABOUT YOUR SOUL PURPOSE

Before we incarnate, our soul chooses a direction for each life. The first step is always to 'wake up', followed by discovering our true role, our Soul Purpose. The term *Soul Purpose* can be misleading as it suggests there is only one outcome. In reality it usually involves multiple gifts, roles or experiences explored at different times. I prefer to view Soul Purpose as a stage in your soul's overall journey rather than a single destination.

Alongside the subtle hints we receive during everyday life to wake up, from a young age we are also given clues to our Soul Purpose. Often called the *Red Thread* in East Asian philosophy, this idea suggests that we can see how seemingly unrelated events in our lives are connected, helping us understand our path and purpose.

The Stages of Awakening

SELF-AWARENESS

The awakening begins when you realize that the things that you were told would make you happy don't actually align with your personal desires. These realizations can be small, like noticing that certain foods negatively affect your mood, or large, such as studying for years to secure a job only to discover it leaves you unfulfilled.

SELF-IMPROVEMENT

Next, you begin to implement changes to your physical and emotional bodies to heal and strengthen them. This can help you feel happier and more in control, but it often leaves a lingering sense that there is still more to life.

SPIRITUAL AWAKENING

Over time you realize these changes only get us so far. This triggers our Spiritual Awakening. From here, we reconnect to our soul and the Universe.

SPIRITUAL DEVELOPMENT

You are now starting to seek meaning at a deeper, soul level. You experience a drive to absorb knowledge and explore personal growth, philosophy and spiritual practices. You can begin to pinpoint the aspects of spirituality and everyday life you enjoy the most and refine those into your Soul Purpose.

ASCENSION

At this stage, you live in alignment with your true, authentic self, operating from a place of pure joy. All souls seek joy, but Lightworkers often intuitively remember the importance of embodying their purpose as fully and quickly as possible.

The Journey from 3D to 5D

In this book, *dimensions* refers to our levels of awareness and how we experience reality. There are three main dimensions and you naturally move up through them in order as your vibration rises. These are:

- **THIRD DIMENSION (3D):** This is the everyday world: where we go to work, pay bills and spend time with friends and family.
- **FOURTH DIMENSION (4D):** This dimension represents transition and change. The realizations that might take place as you progress through this book often take place in 4D.
- **FIFTH DIMENSION (5D):** Once you reach the Spiritual Awakening and Ascension stages, you enter 5D. Here, you can identify your core skills and passions – your Soul Purpose – and live a life aligned with joy. Living in 5D represents the state of consciousness that each soul ultimately aspires to reach.

5D IN THE PAST

Many believe that early humans could not achieve 5D because too much of our focus was on survival.

As humanity evolved, those pursuing a spiritual path often had to separate themselves from their communities and spend extended periods alone. This solitude allowed their energy to rise, giving them access to higher dimensions while remaining in the physical world.

This is why spiritual figures such as Jesus and Buddha famously withdrew to meditate and reflect. By removing themselves from the collective's lower-frequency energy, they could elevate their own energy and connect with the Universe.

Today, the collective frequency is higher, allowing more people to experience these higher dimensions without isolation – a sign that humanity is slowly moving in the right direction.

HOW YOUR REALITY SHIFTS ACROSS DIMENSIONS

CATEGORY	3D LIFESTYLE	4D LIFESTYLE	5D LIFESTYLE
CONSCIOUSNESS	Reality feels fixed. People are attached to ego and physical identity. Global focus on materialism, division and fear.	Begins questioning reality, seeking purpose and exploring spirituality. Energy and emotions are recognized as key influences.	Experiences unity, oneness and unconditional love. Trusts the flow of the Universe and inner guidance. Perceives everything as energy and vibration.
BEHAVIOUR	Driven by societal expectations and approval. Views the world as competitive and judgemental. Focuses on success and status. Often reactive and emotionally triggered.	Self-reflective, curious and open-minded. Focused on healing emotional wounds. Can still operate in 3D but is now conscious of it.	Operates from love, intuition and soul alignment. Prioritizes compassion and non-judgement. Seeks deeper connection with nature, spirit and the Universe.
INTERESTS	Mainstream media, entertainment, money and physical possessions.	Explores self-help, energy work, plant medicine, astrology and soul-searching topics.	Engages in planetary healing, galactic consciousness, telepathy, sacred geometry and purpose- or intuition-driven living.
ACTIVITIES	Career-centred routines.	Yoga, meditation, breathwork, journalling, personal development courses and alternative therapies.	Soul Missions, Lightwork, gridwork, Activations, deep meditation, conscious co-creation and multidimensional travel.
FOOD CHOICES	Convenient, ultra-processed, fast food; sugar-loaded, meat-based or chemically enhanced.	Shift toward vegetarian, organic and conscious eating. Begins tuning into the energy of food.	Intuitive, plant-based, high-vibrational foods chosen for energy alignment.
HEALTHCARE	Guided solely by doctors and drugs. Treats symptoms rather than root causes.	Combines science and spirituality. Uses natural remedies, energy medicine, therapy and intuition alongside conventional healthcare.	Sees the body as a self-healing organism aligned with vibration. Prioritizes using light, sound, frequency and energy fields to heal.

The Earth's Ascension

Gaia is the name given to the soul of our planet, but in some cases she is also seen as Goddess Gaia. For thousands of years, human behaviour has kept Her energy lower, but now we are at a pivotal moment in time: She is determined to make the leap to ascend from 3D to 5D.

To support this ambitious goal, a 'call' went out into the Universe inviting higher vibrational souls, like you, to reincarnate on Earth at this moment. To achieve Ascension, Gaia relies on many of us to first live in the higher dimensions ourselves. This is why it is essential for you to find your joy and embrace the Lightworker path.

While the task may seem daunting, all you need to do to begin is to understand what brings you joy. Living from this positive energy creates a ripple effect, inspiring and awakening others in turn, and helping humanity shift from the heavy energies of fear and separation toward shared frequencies of love, joy and unity. If these emotions were prioritized, everyone would be cared for, including the natural world and Gaia Herself.

So, Lightworker, you are important! While no single person can 'fix' the world, your role is to embody your light and the rest will come. We will explore this in further depth in Chapter 14, when we discuss Double Missions (see pages 177–81).

Light Code Activation: Awakening Your Inner Light

As you begin to find your light, some of what I have shared may start feeling familiar. This is because you may not be learning it for the first time but rather remembering wisdoms from previous lives or ancestral connections. This exercise will help you reconnect with these hidden parts of yourself and gradually invite this understanding back into your consciousness.

The purpose of this Activation is to signal to the Universe that you are ready and open to receive insights. You may experience revelations during the Activation, or they may appear in the days afterward. Take some time to relax in your Activation space before beginning.

ANCIENT STONE CIRCLE MEDITATION

1. Relax with your hands on your heart and imagine yourself on an early morning walk through a forest. Take a moment to notice the sounds, smells and sensations around you.
2. Visualize walking through the forest until the trees break away and open up into a meadow. At the far end there is a gentle incline leading to a stone circle. Walk toward the outside of the circle.
3. Step into the stone circle and lie down.
4. Visualize each of the following items, imagining them turning pink for love as you say their name out loud, followed by the phrase: *remember*:
   - Your physical body
   - The area around your physical body (your energy body)
   - Your home and homelife
   - Your community
   - Places you have lived
   - The world, the solar system and the galaxy.
5. See the vision of yourself in the stone circle, rise up and step outside.
6. Sit atop the slope and enjoy the sunrise. See it as a symbol of new beginnings, and allow that energy to fill you with hope and joy.
7. When you feel ready, bring your awareness to your heart, pause for a moment, and then slowly open your eyes.

CHAPTER 2

Soul Origins and Lightworker Types

'It is the human condition to separate, but you are connected to everything.

You are Galactic.'

– THE AKASHIC RECORDS

Your Soul is Special

Every soul is unique. To understand the complexity of our souls, it's helpful to consider two broad Lightworker soul categories: Earthseeds and Starseeds. Each soul has lived multiple lifetimes, and these terms provide a framework for understanding a soul's journey so that you can discover what kind of Lightworker you are and what your purpose is.

Earthseeds

Earthseeds are souls who have spent most of their incarnations on Earth. They have a deep love for the physical world and truly thrive here on Earth. As Earthseeds move from 3D to 5D awareness (see pages 24–5) and they wake up to their Lightworker gifts, their appreciation for nature and the land becomes increasingly evident. Their natural gifts often include traditional crafts, herbalism, plant medicine, horticulture, ecology, conservation and marine biology.

With numerous lifetimes on Earth, they maintain strong Ancestral connections, honouring traditions and seeking guidance from those who came before. Earthseeds are typically attuned to the rhythms of the seasons, Nature Spirits (guardians of the natural world, normally specific locations) and Elementals (non-physical beings that are connected to the elements).

Starseeds

Those who are not Earthseeds are often Starseeds – souls originating from other star systems. With less experience in 3D life, Starseeds can find Earth challenging, or they feel lonely and out of place. Many struggle with societal systems, conflicts and denser energies on this planet.

Starseed children are often spiritually curious from a young age. They are naturally drawn to metaphysical studies, energy healing and soul-based work. In general, they are highly sensitive beings, strong empaths and deeply intuitive.

Gaia's Call to Starseeds

Gaia has sent out an energetic call to the galaxies, inviting higher vibrational souls to incarnate on Earth and assist in raising its frequency. This invitation came after the destruction of the Second World War. The aim was to help humanity move from cycles of conflict toward more conscious, heart-led living.

By the 1960s, a generational shift became clear: younger people were perceiving the world differently, reflecting the arrival of Starseeds answering Gaia's call. These young people stood out as deeply sensitive, emotionally aware and disconnected from the harsher aspects of human life. Many were highly intuitive, drawn to creativity, healing and spiritual practices from a young age. They carried little Karmic weight and were put here to inspire positive change and help build new systems rooted in unity and higher consciousness.

Starseeds Across Generations

The table below outlines the generational evolution of Starseed Lightworkers from the 1970s onwards.

	STARSEED SOUL TYPE		
	INDIGO CHILDREN	**CRYSTAL CHILDREN**	**RAINBOW CHILDREN**
BIRTH DATE	Started in the 1960s but mostly ranging from 1970s to 1980s.	Mostly 1980s and the 2000s onward.	From the 2010s onward.
PERSONALITY TRAITS	Fiercely independent, psychic, rebellious and truth-seeking.	Gentle, emotionally wise, telepathic, drawn to nature and animals.	High-vibrational, radiant, fearless, minimal Karmic baggage.
SOUL MISSIONS	Challenge authority, break down systems and expose the truth.	Embody divine love and empathy.	Anchor joy and unconditional love.
CHALLENGES	Authority issues, rebuilding education systems and neurodivergence.	Overstimulation, hypersensitivity to sound and light.	Struggles with Earth's density or confusion around purpose.

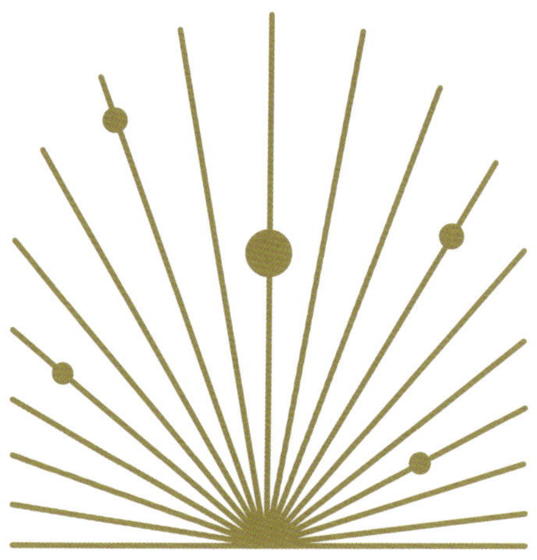

Starseed Origins

This table highlights some of the planetary origins of Starseeds, based on Akashic Records insights. This is not an exhaustive list, but a sample of common origins. You can think of Starseed traits as personality archetypes that influence our learning style, interests, strengths and relationships.

STARSEED NAME/ PLANET OF ORIGIN	COLLECTIVE INTERESTS	PERSONALITY TRAITS
PLEIADIAN	Fifth-dimensional skills. A focus on love, harmony and feminine wisdom.	Natural healers, teachers and Intuitives. Deeply empathetic and heart-centred. Enjoy women's circles and Goddess teachings. May struggle with people-pleasing and over-giving. Long for soul family and a peaceful world.
SIRIAN	Technological innovation, sacred geometry and ancient wisdom.	Intellectually curious, highly analytical, organized, structured, reserved and mysterious. Interested in ancient civilizations. Strong connection to dolphins, whales, water and sound.
ARCTURIAN	Futuristic ideas and multi-dimensional awareness.	Work well in groups, innovative and highly psychic. Interested in alternative realities and new ways to work with energy medicine.
LYRAN	Creative, independent and courageous.	Bold and determined natural leaders. Strong sense of identity and creative expression. Freedom-lovers and independent. Ego may sometimes take charge.
ANDROMEDAN	Freedom, expeditions and deep spiritual development.	Sensitive, observational, freedom-oriented and enjoy exploring. May struggle to commit until their purpose is clear; then they are unstoppable.
ORION	Ancient warriors, mastery of the lessons of polarity.	Desire to understand the Universe, science and philosophy. Often sceptical of spirituality at first. Intensely loyal and protective. Constantly trying to balance heart and mind.

Can We Classify Our Souls that Easily?

While classifications like *Starseed* or *Earthseed* can be helpful, the truth is that our souls are far more complex and multidimensional than any single label can capture. Many souls currently on Earth tend to either reincarnate here regularly or have originated from other realms, but at any point in their journey, a soul may choose to experience a non-human existence – not as an escape but to expand awareness and grow through different forms of consciousness.

Each incarnation leaves an imprint, shaping a soul's personality, wisdom and deeper understanding of the Universe. Every soul is therefore unique. Instead of seeing your soul as fixed to one origin, consider it a multidimensional being, capable of accessing various realms and drawing upon different spiritual lineages to support you in everyday life.

Soul Groups

Each soul is part of a Soul Group, typically composed of close friends and family members we recognize in this life. These groups act as a team of souls working together to create scenarios that facilitate lessons planned for that soul's lifetime. If the Earth is the stage where lessons are learned, your Soul Group plays all the roles. Your soul has also entered a Soul Contract to do the same for them. Most souls have one group, but if they have experienced lives in different places or dimensions, they may connect with multiple Soul Groups.

Soul Pods

Soul Groups are part of a Soul Pod, a larger community of souls who support your everyday life. This includes extended family, teachers, clients and co-workers.

Oversoul

Each Soul Pod is housed in an Oversoul, which is more directly connected to the Universe. Oversouls are overseen by the Council of Twelve (see page 159).

Soul Dynamics

Many lessons on Earth explore polarity, allowing souls to embody the full spectrum of an experience. That means that in one life, you may play a specific role; in the next life, you might play another, helping you and your Soul Group members understand other sides.

Planned moments Soul Groups facilitate may include:

- Triggering your spiritual awakening
- Supporting your growth
- Challenging your limitations
- Mirroring your behaviour back to you
- Working through a lesson with you

These lessons are focused on a soul's overall goal, often referred to as Ascension or entering 5D. Daily life is not pre-planned – only the defining moments and major lessons that progress spiritual development. This perspective can help those who have experienced hardship reframe challenges as meaningful lessons that enrich the soul.

It is also important to remember that once a soul has reincarnated and the veils are in place, their human self has free will to choose its path. This means planned moments might not always take place or unfold as intended. However, your choice to read this book suggests you are waking up and have likely already experienced some of these lessons.

Light Code Activation: Merkabah Integration

The Merkabah is a key symbol in sacred geometry. The two interlocking tetrahedrons form a star tetrahedron believed to be the shape our souls travel to Earth in. It represents the union of body and spirit, masculine and feminine. When we arrive on Earth, the energy of the Merkabah stays with us, however, the veils disconnect us from them. After we lift the veils, we need to actively re-engage.

When we reconnect to our Merkabah it acts as a teacher, helping us become aware of the energies around us, and learning to work consciously with these energies, not against them. In this short Activation, I invite you to reconnect with your Merkabah so it can act as that energetic bridge, helping you remember the wisdoms your soul is ready to remember.

Merkabah Integration

1. Once relaxed, in your mind's eye, imagine an image of yourself.
2. Now imagine a large rainbow-coloured Merkabah, hovering above your head. You might see it moving or vibrating.
3. When you are ready, slowly imagine it moving down so it surrounds you. As it does, you might feel an energetic shift in your physical body.
4. Take a few breaths and then start seeing your Merkabah rotate at a steady pace. This may take a while, but once it's done, your Merkabah is fully integrated.

MERKABAH AS PROTECTION

Visualizing your Merkabah around your body protects your energy field. Therefore, when we learn to connect to your Intuition and Guides, I ask you to imagine your Merkabah first.

PART 2

Understanding Energy and Light

'Up until this moment,
your past was hidden.

This creates the questions
that get you to this moment.

That was their role.'

– THE AKASHIC RECORDS

CHAPTER 3

The Light Body

'You are multifaceted! When you lift the veil, you will see just how much magic you can offer the world!'

– THE AKASHIC RECORDS

Beyond the Physical

Now that we've explored your soul's lineage and the importance of your purpose, you should be beginning to see how living in alignment with your dreams and raising your vibration ripples outwards, transforming not only your life but also the lives of those around you.

Before we can dive fully into the next step of your Lightworker journey, we need to deepen our understanding of the energies that flow within us. These energies are not abstract or distant – they are a key part of who you are. When you learn how to connect with them and influence them, you unlock a powerful foundation for remembrance, growth and expansion.

We are not just a physical body; it is only a small part of us. Beyond our physical bodies lie four energetic layers, always present, but hidden from the naked eye. When the veils are in place, we are only using a fraction of our true abilities. The purpose of these veils is to conceal our greater energetic nature so we can focus on the physical world. Though this may feel limiting, it is intentional as it allows our soul to forget its larger plan and fully engage in the lessons of human life with authenticity.

In this chapter, we will begin to explore the Light Body, your energetic framework and spiritual essence. These teachings will empower you to move forward with greater clarity and confidence, navigating past your metaphorical crossroads with ease.

The Koshas

Although we've been using the term *veil* thus far, the Sanskrit word for this is *Kosha*. The concept of the Koshas originates from Vedic Teachings, and it refers to the idea that we each possess five 'bodies', or layers of varying energy concentrations that encase our pure consciousness.

As pictured below, the four veils separate the five aspects of ourselves. Each aspect is increasingly more energetic.

THE KOSHAS EXPLAINED

ANNAMAYA KOSHA: This is the first aspect of our being, and the one we are most familiar with – our physical body. When all veils are down, our awareness is limited to the physical (3D) world and our physical body. Healing can only be focused on the physical body.

PRANAMAYA KOSHA: Also known as the Energy Body, when the next layer lifts we get to experience the flow of life-force energy through the body. Although it does this work when the veil is down, once it lifts, we become aware of how we feel if we make a high-frequency choice, compared to a low-frequency choice.

Practices like Reiki or Qi Gong can help you interact with your energy body and understand how to support your physical body through it.

MANOMAYA KOSHA: When the third veil lifts, we gain more insight into our Emotional Body. This Kosha is subtle so you might not notice this layer lifting. We experience energy in our body mainly as emotions so once the third layer lifts and we connect to our Manomaya Kosha, those emotions help us understand what is going on in our energy body. The Emotional Body teaches us that our perceptions shape our reality and the emotions that show up give us clues to the energy healing we should do.

VIJNANAMAYA KOSHA: Acknowledging and deliberately supporting our emotional and energy body helps us to connect to our Vijñānamaya Kosha, our Intuitive Body. This body allows us to communicate directly with our Higher Self (our soul when we are in a physical body), guiding us towards what brings us joy (our Soul Purpose).

ANANDAMAYA KOSHA: When lifted, this final veil grants us access to Anandamaya Kosha or the Bliss Body (the soul). Once you are connected to its energy, you are as closely linked to the Universe as you can be. At this point, you and your soul are one again, helping you become fully aligned with your purpose. It means you can comprehend that you are a soul first, here in the physical world to learn lessons. Once all bodies are fully integrated, that means we are living from our soul's energy, which is the 5D lifestyle our soul wants us to reach.

We can go through life and achieve goals without reconnecting to these hidden aspects of ourselves. However, the awakening process is the path our souls want us to take, as it means we focus on our true goals and work towards them, free from any actions that would be detrimental to others.

The lifting of the veils is significant for a Lightworker, as their skills are often found within the hidden layers. For example, Energy Healers will be working with the Emotional Body and Energy Body. To heighten their psychic skills, Intuitives will experience significant shifts when they reconnect to the Intuitive Body and at the same time, Lightworkers in other industries will be inspired to find innovative 5D ways to work as they reconnect to all layers.

Dr Lucy's story is a clear example of someone who started in a highly admired 3D career, which focused on the physical body, but over time her journey expanded.

DR LUCY – REDEFINING SUCCESS AND FOLLOWING HER SOUL'S COMPASS

A Career That Wasn't the Right Fit

Lucy doesn't regret studying medicine. The years of training shaped her, but after six years at university and a decade practising, she realized it simply wasn't for her.

Early in her career, she looked up the hierarchical ladder of medicine, expecting things to get better. Instead, she saw stressed-out Registrars and burned-out Consultants. Eventually, she made the decision that many of her peers only dreamed of: she left!

It struck her how some of the brightest, most highly qualified people on the planet could feel so trapped, as though their skills couldn't possibly apply anywhere else. Her answer is simple: *'No matter how stuck, scared or sick you feel emotionally, physically or deep in your soul, if something no longer feels aligned, you have to leave.'*

A New Path Guided by Spirit

Since leaving medicine, Lucy has built a life grounded in spiritual practice, guided by her intuition. Essential oils, crystals, energy work and a deep connection to the natural world are now her daily companions.

To some, this might sound strange. To Lucy, that doesn't matter: *'You do it anyway. That's the assignment.'* She trusts that the Universe provides her with opportunities she never imagined – she just needs to take the next aligned step.

LUCY'S MESSAGE:

1. Keep your soul front and centre: that connection is your compass.
2. Trust the next step: you don't need the whole plan.
3. Define success for yourself: only you decide what feels like home.

KEY TAKEAWAY: Your past doesn't define your purpose. When something stops feeling like home, you have the power and the responsibility to walk the path meant for you.

Diving into Pranamaya Kosha – The Energy Body

We will now focus on the first body that becomes available to us, Pranamaya Kosha.

Once the first veil lifts, we reconnect to the Energy Body. This is a non-physical part of ourselves and it consists of life-force energy (often called Chi, Prana or Qi). We might experience the Energy Body through sensations like tingling, warmth or a sense of expansion or contraction during practices like meditation, breathwork or yoga.

Just as our physical body is made up of many functions, the Energy Body has its own set of systems, including Meridian Lines, Nadis and the chakras. Together, these energies combine to create our Aura, which is shaped like a sphere around the body. When you walk into a room and pick up on a 'bad vibe', that is your Aura sending you a warning message.

Why Is It Essential to Look After Our Energy Body?

Energy Medicine teaches two important points. Physical ailments often result from unaddressed emotion, such as trauma, which is held in the body, potentially leaving an area of weakness in the Energy Body. Once this happens, there is the potential for more emotions, big or small, to impact that same area, creating a denser energy build-up until the point it manifests in the physical body.

Secondly, our physical body has the lowest frequency of the five layers – that translates to healing being a slower process when we focus on that area. In contrast, Energy Healing focuses on supporting and correcting the Energy Body. As those improvements can happen faster in the energy, and as each layer is linked, those changes feed through into the physical body.

The Chakras

The chakra system is the most useful aspect of our Energy Body for Lightworkers to explore because it allows us to understand how life events really affect us and how we may overcome them. This is why we are going to look at the classic chakras, as well as the relevant Higher Chakras.

An Introduction to the Chakras

The role of the chakras is to filter the energies and emotions we experience, before storing or releasing them. Many believe there are more chakras but for now we will focus on the seven main ones. These are discs of energy running up the spine, through the head, to the crown. A line of energy, known as the Line of Liberation, runs up the body, through each chakra.

As we grow and learn, more of these chakras become available to us. Each chakra represents an area of the body, as well as specific life stages and lessons we explore at that age. The final one to open is the Crown Chakra, which offers our spiritual lessons.

A fully-open, healthy chakra is known as a 'Balanced Chakra'. In this case, energy runs through it with ease and the chakra itself should have a steady, slow rotation. Over time, various events and experiences can deplete a disc, resulting in reduced or no energy; sometimes stopping the spin altogether. Alternatively, too much energy in a disc, known as an 'Overactive Chakra' increases its intensity and spin. Blocked or overactive chakras can then start to affect the flow of energy (*prana*) running through the body, showing up as all kinds of emotional or physical ailments as well as obstacles affecting our ability to manifest and achieve our goals.

Each chakra vibrates at a different frequency and since colours are also a form of vibration, as illustrated in the image overleaf, each chakra has a corresponding colour. To heal the Energy Body and specifically the chakras, we use complementary frequencies to correct the flow of energy. The aim is to bring a chakra back into balance.

Overleaf are a diagram and table showing all the primary chakras, where they are placed on the body, the issues connected to each chakra and the colour(s) each one is connected to.

The Primary Chakras

CHAKRAS	BEHAVIOURS THAT REFLECT A HEALTHY CHAKRA	BEHAVIOURS THAT SHOW AN UNDERACTIVE OR OVERACTIVE CHAKRA	CHAKRA COLOUR(S)
CROWN	Spiritually connected, universal love and consciousness. Intelligent, open-minded, questioning and receives information. Aware, wise and understanding.	Rigid belief systems, critical of spirituality, weak faith, depression, apathy, learning difficulties, anger at the Universe, loneliness.	White, Clear and Violet
THIRD EYE	Imaginative, intuitive and perceptive. Good memory, assimilates information, clear thoughts and vision. Able to see beyond the physical.	Poor imagination, memory or judgement. Polarized views, denial, polarized, insensitive and can't see beyond the physical.	Purple
THROAT	Confident and able communicator, expressive, good listener, good sense of timing and rhythm.	Inability to express oneself or speak out, misunderstood, secretive, not a good listener. Low voice level, shy, tone deaf or poor rhythm.	Blue
HEART	Peaceful, balanced, loving, compassionate, empathetic, tolerant, altruistic or forgiving.	Heart-broken, lack of empathy, bitter, rejected, conditional love, hateful, antisocial, isolated and intolerant.	Green or Pink
SOLAR PLEXUS	Confident, warm, good energy levels, responsible, reliable or spontaneous. Good sense of humour, drive and personal power.	Low self-esteem, feeling powerless, easily manipulated, poor self-discipline, unreliable, inferiority complex, imposter syndrome, cold or low energy.	Yellow
SACRAL	Healthy relationships with self and others. Emotional intelligence, passionate, healthy libido, good boundaries, creative, graceful movement.	Poor social skills, lack of passion or creativity. Unhealthy relationships, codependency, attachment, excessive boundaries. Low libido, fear of sex or intimacy, sexual trauma or addiction.	Orange
ROOT	Does not mind change. Enjoys and trusts life, feels safe, secure and stable. Is grounded and comfortable in their body.	Fearful, anxious, restless, poor boundaries, financial difficulties, disorganized, poor discipline, disconnected from the body, neglects self, not grounded.	Red, Black, Brown, Metallic, Earthy colours

Crown Chakra
Third Eye Chakra
Throat Chakra
Heart Chakra
Solar Plexus Chakra
Sacral Chakra
Root Chakra

The Higher Chakras

Once the seven primary chakras have opened and the veils have been lifted, we can access the Higher Chakras. These have more advanced 5D themes related to our Ascension process. The image below highlights the placement of the Higher Chakras and the table opposite explains the colour, position and energies of each. These chakras are useful for a Lightworker's lifestyle and will be the subject of several of our Activations.

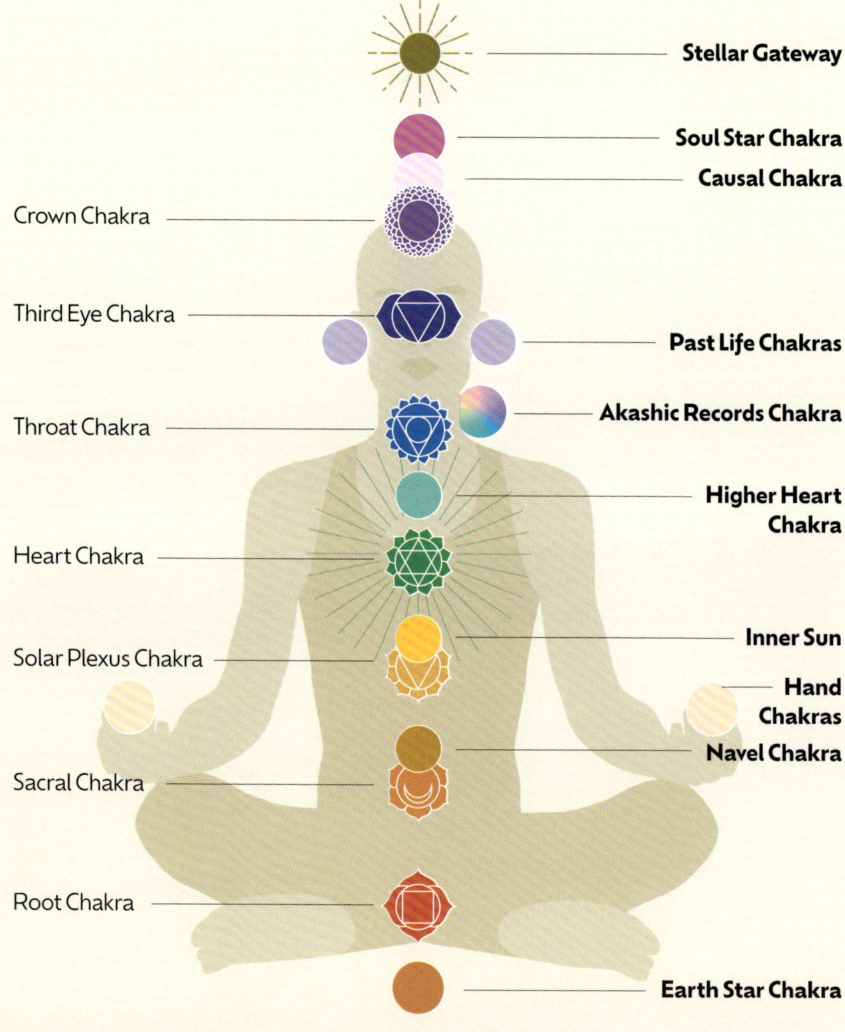

The Higher Chakras

HIGHER CHAKRA	POSITION	PROPERTIES/USES	COLOUR
STELLAR GATEWAY	Two metres (6ft) above the Crown.	Connecting us to the Galaxies and everything out there.	Pearlescent gold
SOUL STAR CHAKRA	One metre (3ft) above the Crown.	This is your Higher Self, the aspect of your soul that is too large and higher frequency to fit into a physical body.	Pearlescent magenta
CAUSAL CHAKRA	In line with but behind the Crown Chakra.	Filters higher vibrational energies before they enter the Crown so you can channel higher frequency information.	White/ Soft cream
PAST LIFE CHAKRAS	Behind each ear.	Offers past life insights.	Pale violet
AKASHIC RECORDS CHAKRA	Back of the neck.	Connects you to your Akashic Records information.	Rainbow light
HIGHER HEART CHAKRA	Between the Heart and Throat Chakra, over the Thymus.	The higher vibrational aspect of the Heart Chakra. It is a bridge between the Heart and Throat Chakra; helping us communicate with diplomacy and live from a state of empathy, compassion and altruism.	Turquoise
HAND CHAKRAS	Over the palms of the hand.	Both these chakras channel healing energies and support those working with their hands. Particularly those in the arts.	White light
INNER SUN	Over the solar plexus.	The higher vibrational aspect of the solar plexus, the Inner Sun, helps us embody our true essence and realize our purpose free from insecurities and fears of what others will think.	Gold
NAVEL CHAKRA	Slightly above but crossing over the Sacral Chakra.	Originally connected to the Sacral Chakra, this chakra reminds us where our soul came from and connects us back to universal consciousness.	Pearlescent orange
EARTH STAR CHAKRA	One metre (3ft) beneath our feet.	Grounds and connects us to Earth and everything we share this planet with.	Pearlescent earthy tones

Light Code Activation: Activating Your Energy Body

Now that you understand the importance of lifting the veils and looking after the seven main chakras, this Activation will help you remove any final veils that might still be in place. We will also focus on each of the seven main chakras, devoting time to each one so we can start moving them back into balance. It's essential to do this work early so that all of the Higher Chakras energies are available to you.

This is an important Activation that will prepare the physical and energetic body for a higher frequency lifestyle. Therefore, you must do this work on a day when you're able to rest so the energies have time to integrate.

Removing the Veil

1. When you are relaxed, imagine four linen sheets placed in a row moving away from you. Hold the intention that each represents a veil that needs to be removed. Think of each one in turn, engage with it, then see it lift up and disappear:

   SHEET ONE: Separating us from our Energy Body and our abilities to access and work with life-force energy.

   SHEET TWO: Separating us from our Emotional Body and our abilities to have control over the mind and choosing positive thoughts.

   SHEET THREE: Separating us from our Intuitive Body and our abilities to receive guidance from our Higher Self and other sources of channelled wisdom.

   SHEET FOUR: Separating us from the ability to live from our soul's energy and connect to the Universe.

2. Once all sheets have been removed, relax for a few moments before continuing with the next steps.

Balancing the Chakras

Now it's time to activate and balance the seven main chakras, clearing any unwanted energies that might have built up:

3. Imagine a multi-coloured light coming up to your feet, then moving up your legs and hips.
4. You are now going to imagine it passing each of the seven main chakras (see page 49 for positions). When it does, visualize a beam of light coming out of the front and back of your body. Hold that visualization for a minute or two before moving to the next chakra.
5. For the Crown Chakra, imagine the coloured lights beaming out of the top of your head.
6. Now imagine that light reducing, travelling back down the chakras until it comes out of your feet and back into the ground.
7. Relax for a few more moments before you open your eyes.

CHAPTER 4

The Energy Around You

'Unlike others, Lightworkers live as energy beings in a physical world. You know you are light first and that means you perceive the world as it really is.'

– THE AKASHIC RECORDS

Tapping Into Energy

Some of the concepts explored so far may feel too esoteric or otherworldly but I'm inviting you to release judgement and embrace what resonates. That quiet knowing stirring inside you recognizes the truth even when your mind can't explain it. This is your soul remembering the wisdoms it already knows; its light guiding you forward, through this crossroads moment. It takes courage to walk a path that may set you apart and step into the unknown, but you've already chosen it, and that choice alone shows the strength of your soul.

Up until now, we've focused on you – your soul origins and the ways you hold and embody energy. But you are not separate from the greater forces of life. To truly understand your purpose, you must also understand the energies you live amongst and the laws that govern them.

We will start by exploring the conscious, subconscious and superconscious mind – the three levels of awareness through which you can work with energy most effectively. Next, we will explore the energies that shape the world around you. We will then turn to the Seven Hermetic Principles, timeless truths that reveal the hidden architecture of reality, before discussing the dimensions of existence, from the mineral, plant and animal kingdoms to the etheric and cosmic planes. Next, we turn to the Laws of the Universe, and from there, we'll touch on quantum understandings of energy and vibration, bridging science and spirituality.

These aren't just spiritual theories; they are the very frameworks through which transformation becomes possible. By the end of this chapter, you'll see how Lightworkers are uniquely attuned to these forces, and how working with them consciously allows you to create rapid, lasting change – not just for yourself, but for the collective.

The Conscious, Subconscious and Superconscious Mind

I'm now going to introduce one of the wisest and fundamental Lightworker superpowers, and that is their deep connection to their intuition. These are skills we will be waking up and developing together. If you don't feel intuitive, I promise you that you are. It's all about identifying the intuitive skills you have.

Many intuitive insights come directly from our Higher Self (see page 43) – the wisest part of us and a part that is tapped into something greater. So why is it more important to listen to our intuition than our conscious or subconscious mind? To answer that question, I first need to break down what each of these is. The iceberg in the illustration opposite highlights how these three aspects of our mind work together.

The conscious mind is above the water line; it is responsible for our everyday tasks and thinking. It focuses on our surroundings, enabling real-time interaction with the world and is responsible for logical analysis and problem-solving. Because it is so busy focusing on what we are doing in any given moment, it is only capable of short-term memory.

The subconscious mind is illustrated by the rest of the iceberg hidden below the surface. Here, emotions, habits and learned experiences are stored. From birth to around the age of seven, children absorb information directly into their subconscious without critical analysis, including negative thought patterns such as fears and limiting beliefs. Because this happens at such an early age, they can be stored as a truth and children can grow up to believe *I'm not worthy*, or perhaps become an adult who fears failure.

Then we have our superconscious mind, represented by the vast ocean of water around the iceberg. This water is representative of the wisdoms available to us through intuitive insights received from the other planes. Therefore, unlike our conscious and subconscious which are both dealing with the present and processing the past, the superconscious is available to us solely for guidance and its connection to something greater. This is why it is the aspect we should be listening to when we need support.

'What we know is a drop, what we don't know is an ocean.'

– ISAAC NEWTON

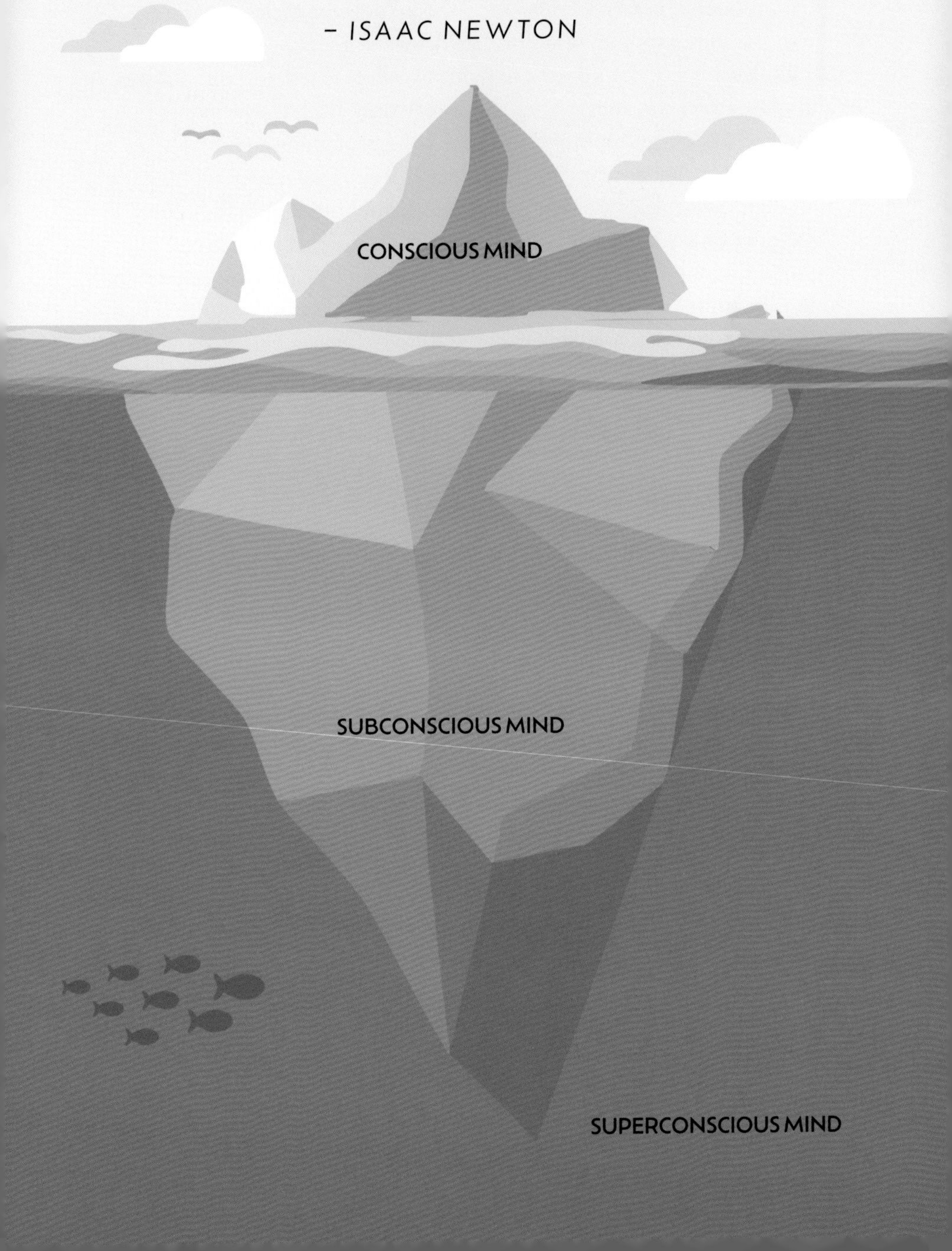

CONSCIOUS MIND

SUBCONSCIOUS MIND

SUPERCONSCIOUS MIND

Seasonal and Lunar Energies

In my book, *The Crystal Almanac*, I shared how the cycles of nature – the seasons, astrology and lunar rhythms – shape the energies around us. These natural shifts exist to guide us: when to rest and turn inward and when to act and engage with the outer world. Each season has its own elemental influence that builds to a peak before softening and dissolving.

This means that not every uncomfortable feeling you experience is truly your own. Sometimes the energy you are sensing comes from the collective rhythm of nature itself. For Lightworkers, these fluctuations can feel especially strong. The good news is that when you recognize the source, the intensity often softens. Simply witnessing these energies and allowing them to move through can bring relief and healing.

SEASONAL ENERGIES AT A GLANCE

SPRING (EARTH): Growth, planning and grounding into the physical world.

SUMMER (FIRE): Action, manifestation and joyful expansion.

AUTUMN (WATER): Reflection, harvest and emotional healing.

WINTER (AIR): A time of stillness, contemplation and rest.

By attuning to these rhythms, you begin to understand that life is cyclical. If emotions feel overwhelming, remember they may ease as the season naturally shifts.

The Moon's Influence

Alongside the seasons, the Moon adds another powerful layer. The New and Full Moons are the most noticeable phases, each stirring emotions and sparking growth. These surges aren't random – they are our regular invitations to reflect, release and realign.

NEW MOON: Marks fresh beginnings. Its energy builds for a few days, amplifying the themes of the zodiac sign it falls in. It's a potent time to set intentions.

FULL MOON: Shines light on what needs to be seen. Its influence is shorter but often more dramatic, bringing clarity, release or breakthroughs.

These lunar energies can trigger sudden waves of emotion, both uplifting and uncomfortable. If you notice yourself feeling heightened around the Moon cycles, try not to judge it. Instead, recognize that the energy is passing through and will soon settle.

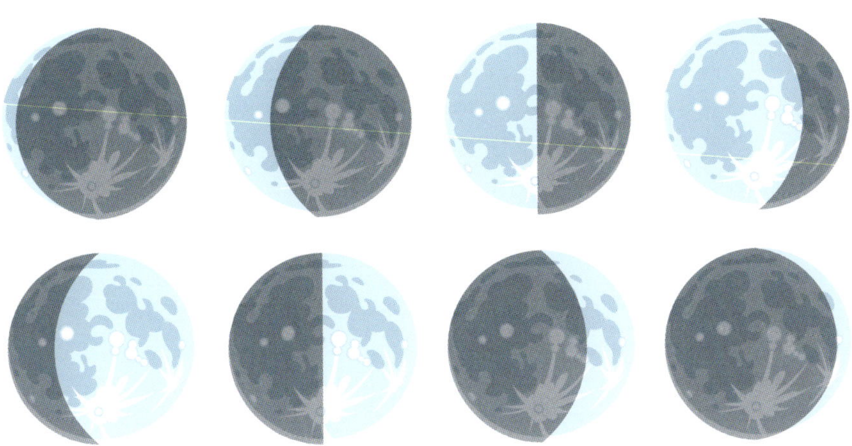

The Seven Hermetic Principles

Hermeticism is an ancient philosophical and esoteric tradition based on the teachings of Hermes Trismegistus, a legendary figure believed to be a fusion of the Greek God Hermes and the Egyptian God Thoth. The title Trismegistus or 'Thrice Great Hermes' reflects his mastery of Alchemy, Astrology and Theurgy.

One of the most well-known texts attributed to this lineage is *The Kybalion*, published anonymously in 1908 by a group calling themselves 'The Three Initiates'. It refined Hermetic wisdom into seven core principles.

These principles offer a universal road map to understanding both the seen and unseen worlds. They give insights into how reality might operate and also how we, as spiritual beings, can align with cosmic law to experience greater clarity, empowerment and transformation.

1. **THE PRINCIPLE OF MENTALISM:** *The All is Mind; the Universe is Mental:* Your mental state shapes your reality. Quantum physics has found that atoms only respond in an expected way when they are observed. This implies that, in every moment, change or healing is possible if we expect to see it happen. This honours a key Energy Medicine concept: the healer does not do the healing, but rather holds space and the intention (the Law of Intention) that they will see a healing.

2. **THE PRINCIPLE OF CORRESPONDENCE:** *As above, so below; as below, so above:* This can imply it is possible to have Heaven on Earth if we choose. It also suggests that what we see on a micro scale is also reflected on a macro scale. For example, chaos in your outer environment may reflect inner chaos and vice versa. If you want to change your outer life, you must begin with inner work – healing your thoughts, emotions and intentions.

3. **THE PRINCIPLE OF VIBRATION:** *Nothing rests; everything moves; everything vibrates:* This highlights the importance of maintaining a high personal frequency through positive thoughts, emotions, nutrition and environments as you attract experiences that match your frequency.

4. THE PRINCIPLE OF POLARITY: *Everything is dual; everything has poles; everything has its pair of opposites:* For example, love and hate are two ends of the same spectrum. It's possible to shift from hate to love by changing your perspective and internal state. Understanding this principle allows you to transform a negative state into a positive one. When a soul is choosing to reincarnate, it works with its Soul Group to decide the polarity of experiences they want to create together.

5. THE PRINCIPLE OF RHYTHM: *Everything flows, out and in; everything has its tides:* You may experience periods of high motivation and creativity, followed by times of rest or low energy. Nature shows this in seasons; spring's growth follows winter's dormancy. We have explored how the different energies around us affect our bodies and emotions.

6. THE PRINCIPLE OF CAUSE AND EFFECT: *Every cause has its effect; every effect has its cause:* Your current habits (causes) are directly responsible for your health, relationships and career outcomes (effects). This lesson asks that we live intentionally. You will remember that these realizations start the process of self-awareness.

7. THE PRINCIPLE OF GENDER: *Gender is inherent in everything; everything possesses both Masculine and Feminine Principles.* Masculine energy is characterized by action, logic and willpower, while feminine energy is marked by intuition, receptivity and nurturing. The lesson here is to honour both, so goal setting needs both strategic action (masculine) and emotional and intuitive intelligence (feminine).

The Dimensions of Existence

'If you want to find the secrets of the Universe, think in terms of energy, frequency and vibration.' – NIKOLA TESLA

We will now explore the different dimensions (seen and unseen) that exist on or are connected to our planet in order to understand the structure and the different energies we can work with.

THE MINERAL KINGDOM: We start with the densest frequency on this planet, the Mineral Kingdom. This is predominantly represented by the crystals and rocks that make up our planet and the landscapes that we live in. These minerals are the building blocks of the plant and animal kingdoms; for this reason, many suggest that crystals have some form of consciousness. In Chapter 5, we will explore essential oils and crystals as Lightworker energy tools.

THE PLANT KINGDOM: If we now bring in carbon, the Plant Kingdom is created. Providing food, the oxygen we breathe and supporting our atmosphere, the Plant Kingdom helps us thrive.

If a psychic wanted to communicate with a plant, they would usually connect with the spirit of a species rather than an individual plant. The elementals, alongside the Fairy Kingdom, support and care for our plants.

THE ANIMAL KINGDOM: This includes human beings. All animals are sentient beings, but their level of awareness and behaviours will affect their frequency. A majority of animals live in the 5D – this shows how one category or Kingdom can host several different frequencies (dimensions).

Etheric Plane

This is where all our souls, human and animal, go between lives. Once a life has ended, souls rest for a short period of time. Reunited with their Akashic Records Reader, their soul friends and those they miss from the life they just left. Then they head to the great classrooms. This is where they go to evaluate the life they just experienced and start planning their next life with their Soul Group.

Time in this dimension goes much faster than on Earth so they can spend a lifetime in the Etheric Plane and yet it might be a few decades or less on Earth. When you connect to your Ancestors, this is the plane you are connecting to.

Cosmic Plane

This is the dimension that hosts all energies that no longer need to incarnate or do not have to. This plane is broken down into frequencies that get incrementally higher. Starting with the Ascended Masters, such as Jesus and Buddha, beings that once took physical form. They stay closely connected to Earth to support the Ascension of others. Then we also have the Councils of Twelve and the Angelic Realm.

Laws of the Universe

This plane holds the blueprint to everything. From here, the structure of the Universe is dictated through a multitude of different laws. Some of these laws are obvious, like the need for gravity and water for life to exist on Earth. However, sacred geometry, for example the mathematics of the Universe, is less obvious.

Then we have many laws that present themselves as potential lessons we might learn on Earth. These include: the Law of Manifestation, Intention and Attraction. As you can imagine, understanding how these laws work can be very empowering so we will explore this in more detail very soon.

The Akashic Records reside on this plane, which means when we connect into the records, we are receiving guidance from the closest frequency possible to the Universe. Here we have the energy that made our soul and the Kingdoms we have spoken about. It also constructed the Laws of the Universe, which then house everything else.

Trusting the Flow

Seasonal and lunar shifts are just two examples of the many unseen energies that move around us. Daily cycles, astrological alignments or even collective world events can ripple through our emotional field. By bringing awareness to these patterns, we may remember that much of what we feel is not permanent and not always personal.

The next time you're caught in a wave of emotion, pause and ask *Is this mine, or is it simply energy moving through?* Trust that, just like the tides, it will eventually calm and as it does – you may discover a sense of peace and empowerment in knowing you are always part of something greater.

Quantum Work

One of the strengths most Lightworkers share is their natural ability to explore abstract and multidimensional ideas. For this reason, many Lightworkers are also aware that every soul is unique. Although society tries to place us in boxes, it quickly becomes clear we were never meant to fit into them.

We know this understanding is often what brings Lightworkers to their metaphorical crossroads. Each of us is the sum total of our soul's journey, not just from this lifetime but from all the lives and realms we have experienced before. Every person carries a unique energetic signature, a frequency shaped by their past, their soul lineage and their purpose. What feels right for one person may not align at all for another. This truth sits at the very heart of Quantum Healing.

Quantum work recognizes that we are all energy – but not identical expressions of energy. It honours our differences, allowing space to consider who we are across different timelines and dimensions. It understands that healing and then change must meet us where *we* are, not where society wants us to be. This awareness isn't just a Lightworker's superpower; it's a gateway to greater compassion and understanding. It helps us understand that we are each living in our own unique reality, shaped by our beliefs and the stories we carry.Taking on a quantum perspective of all things, as often as we can, helps us to stay open-minded, to consider that other dimensions and unseen influences may be at play in our healing journey. Interestingly, Quantum Healing also believes change doesn't have to be linear or slow. In the quantum field, transformation can happen in an instant.

As we move forward, you'll hear the word 'quantum' come up regularly. Let it serve as a reminder:

You are not just a physical being. You are a multidimensional, energetic soul, capable of fast, deep and lasting change; especially when you work alongside the Universe, not against it.

Light Code Activation: Calling Back All Lost Soul Fragments

Life-altering or traumatic experiences can fragment your soul's energy and then, over several lifetimes, this energy can become depleted. On your journey to understanding who you really are, it can be helpful to draw back any energies lost in previous lifetimes so that you can move forward as your whole self.

Inspired by the Star of David, the following crystal layout Activation rebalances the elements in your body and re-establishes your connection to Heaven, where we go between lives, and Earth. It works because each point of the crystal faces your body, redirecting energies you may have lost back to you.

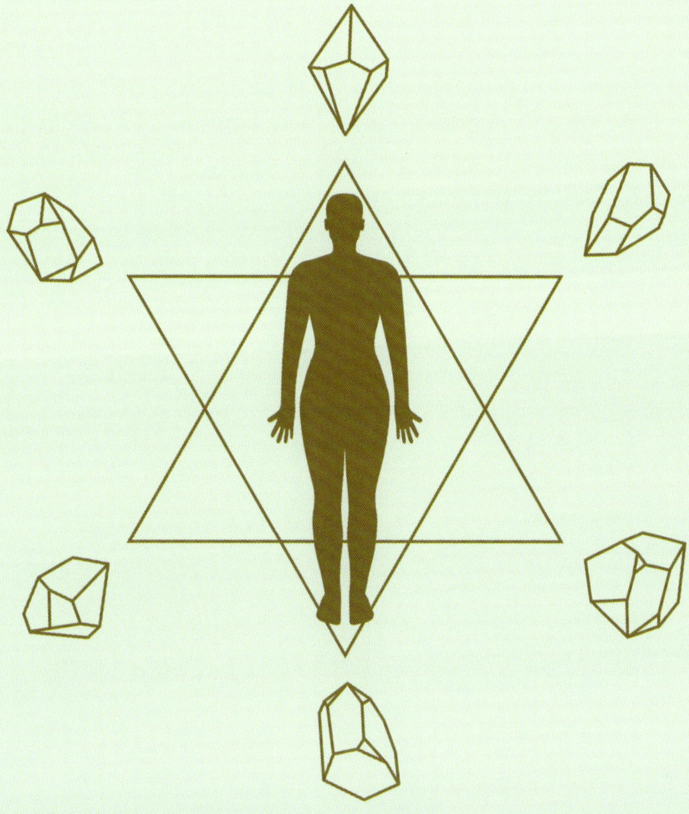

Solomon Seal Crystal Healing

1. Source six clear quartz points of any size. Arrange the six points into a star, large enough for you to lie in the centre, with all points facing inward.
2. Lie comfortably in the centre of the star. With absolute conviction, state five times: *I claim back any energies I have lost in this life.*
3. Relax, take several deep breaths, then state: *I claim back any energies I have lost in Past Lives.*
4. Pause, breathe deeply and state: *I claim back any energies I have lost from all other possible lives or dimensions.*
5. Remain in this position for 15 minutes, breathing deeply and visualizing your energy returning to you.
6. Close the Activation by sitting up and removing the crystal points, starting with the one above the head.
7. Wait a moment and then stand up.

CHAPTER 5

Energy Tools for Lightworkers

'Humans do not need to create new tools. What you need, nature has always provided.'

– THE AKASHIC RECORDS

The Importance of Energy Tools

We have learned that we are more energy than physical matter; now it is time to learn about the different energy tools at our disposal. Energy tools allow us to work directly with the energetic layers of our being, supporting faster and more effective remembering, healing and Ascension. These tools can be objects or techniques, and you can use them to move, clear, balance and amplify energy within your body, aura or environment. Think of them as frequency holders, each carrying the vibration needed to support a specific energetic shift or transformation.

First, we will focus on the energy tools most commonly used by Lightworkers: crystals and essential oils. Together we will discover when to use them, how to integrate them into your practice and how to tailor their use to your unique needs as you walk the path.

Crystals as Energy Tools

Crystal Healing has been a passion of mine for decades and was the topic of my three previous books: *The Crystal Apothecary*, *Your Crystal Plan* and *The Crystal Almanac*. The techniques that I am going to teach you, I have been practising for years, so I know their potential. I also know the joy it brings Lightworkers when they see the results.

Each type of crystal has its unique frequency (its healing energy). Their colour is a clue to the overarching themes of different crystals. (*Hint:* the colour themes match the themes of each chakra.) Within that overarching theme, each crystal type has a unique frequency that gives it its healing properties.

In contrast, humans are composed of multiple atomic structures, which means we emit a wide range of frequencies. When stressed, it is harder and takes longer to calm our energies.

Science shows that as we have a lower frequency, when we bring a higher frequency crystal close to us it raises our vibration, dispelling unwanted energies as they go. This is why they are the perfect energy tool. They are taking unwanted energies away from us in a calm, subtle way. Within moments the crystal's frequency will stabilize.

Since crystals have specific frequencies, we can select the exact ones to raise our vibration above unwanted energy we want to heal, such as negative emotions. We can then use crystals to help us manifest by raising our vibration towards the things we want to bring into our lives, such as our goals and dreams and in this case, our journey towards our purpose. The Activation in this chapter is my Healing Protocol. This is an energy medicine practice I invite you to learn and use for each memory, emotion or energy you have noted down as something that needs lifting from your body.

Ongoing Crystal Support

Each healing will require a crystal that matches the theme of the work you are doing. At the end of this book is a collection of the ideal crystal supports (see pages 186–7), plus a master Healing Crystal you can use for all of them.

Once you have done the protocol to ensure the deep healing is happening, I would suggest you seal the healing in by using your chosen crystal in one of the following ways.

Crystal Elixirs

Water infused with the energy of a crystal. This allows you to ingest the frequency of a crystal, making it particularly useful when wanting to support the physical body. To create an elixir, simply place your chosen crystal next to a glass of drinking water for at least 20 minutes. Then sip the water very slowly.

Carrying a Crystal with You

When we wear or carry a crystal with us, its energies become more integrated into our energy field, helping embed the healing work more deeply. I would suggest placing the crystal away from you at night so your energies can rest.

Displaying Crystals in Your Home

Displaying a crystal in the home allows you to connect to its healing energy at regular intervals throughout the day. Place it in a room where you perform tasks that match the crystal's properties. However, take it out of the bedroom at night to ensure a good night's sleep.

CHOOSING YOUR CRYSTAL

When sourcing crystals, the size and shape are not important. Instead, please pick the crystal that almost energetically waves at you. That is an intuitive sign it is the right one.

Essential Oils as Energy Tools

We are all unique and drawn to different things. Therefore, I wanted to give you two energy tool options. Both crystals and essential oils can be used for our protocol and both are equally successful, so it comes down to personal preference.

Essential oils are the pure, concentrated aromatic compounds naturally found within plants. To offer the most impact, they need to be steam-distilled or cold-pressed. Each oil carries the distinctive essence of its source, whether it comes from flowers, leaves, roots or rind.

When we inhale essential oils, their aromatic molecules travel through the nose and stimulate the olfactory system, which is the part of the brain connected to smell. This system is directly linked to the limbic region, which plays a key role in regulating emotions, memory, heart rate and stress levels.

Therefore as long as you are using pure oils (non adulterated and free from fillers and synthetics) when inhaled, the oils enter the lungs and then the bloodstream, accessing and supporting each cell in the body. We know the emotional body supports the physical body; essential oils are literally breathed in, supporting the mind and our emotions first, they then head to every cell in the body.

THE LIGHTWORKER EMOTIONAL FIRST AID KIT

In the future, when you have gone through a shock or can feel emotions bubbling up, bring in the relevant essential oil. They are perfect at helping process emotions in the moment, so they don't get trapped in the body. For guidance on which crystals and essential oils to use, feel free to send me a message directly on Instagram: @crystalmysteryschool.

Using Oils Aromatically

Essential oils are very easy to use. You might choose to simply inhale the oil from the bottle, and that would be sufficient. You could add them to your clothes, like a perfume, or do the following:

1. Add one or two drops of oil to the palms of your hands.
2. Rub them together (avoid getting them on your fingers as you don't want to rub the oils into your eye accidentally).
3. Close your eyes and cup your palms over your nose.
4. Take in two to three deep breaths.

It is as easy as that! This is the four-step process I suggest doing during the protocol and is something you might want to do afterwards to continue the healing. There is a chance you won't like every oil's smell, but remember, you're not meant to love every scent. It's about using the one that offers you the healing you need.

Inhaling Essential Oils Safely

When appropriate levels are used in well-ventilated spaces, essential oil inhalation is a mostly safe and effective way to enjoy the benefits of essential oils. However, if you have a sensitivity to essential oils, sensitive skin (or fear you might), you can inhale the oils directly from the bottle. While it is uncommon, some oils are not for inhalation, so always read the labels and follow guidelines.

Diffusing Oils

Using a diffuser to disperse the oils around the room allows you to breathe them in throughout the day or while sleeping. Always use a cold plate diffuser rather than a tealight diffuser, which burn off the oils before they are released into the air.

The amount of oil diffused, proximity to the diffuser and size of the room will determine how long an oil should be diffused. For a cold plate diffuser, it's generally recommended to use two to four drops of oil per diffusion period. Larger amounts are used exclusively for larger spaces.

When diffusing around babies, children, pregnant women, the elderly or pets, keep the dosage low and the space ventilated. Leave doors open for pets so they can choose to leave the space.

Connecting with Your Crystals and Oils

The best way to understand how you should work with a crystal or oil is by connecting to its energies and asking it directly. To do this, hold either the crystal or oil bottle in the hand you write with. If the crystal is too large or heavy to pick up, simply sit next to it and place your hand on it. Then follow the steps below:

1. Protect your energies, then imagine a cloak energetically falling down and wrapping around you. This is the Cloak of Truth and Love. It prevents any misguided intuitive messages reaching us.
2. Take a few moments to move your hands over the bottle or crystal so you are really engaging with it. In your mind's eye, consider what it feels like: is it rough or smooth, heavy or light? Can you feel any imperfections?
3. Then, on a slow inhale, ask each of the following questions. Open up all your senses and see what information comes on the exhale.
   - *Do you have a message for me?*
   - *I've been drawn to work with you for ...*
   - *Can we start that work today?*
   - *Which technique should I use?*
   - *How regularly can I work with you?*
   - *Is there any additional guidance you can offer?*
4. Once you have finished asking your questions, send gratitude to your crystal or oil. Then put it down.
5. Open your eyes and note down anything you want to remember.

CLEANSING YOUR CRYSTALS AND OILS

To cleanse any pent-up energies from your crystal or oil bottle, hold it in your hands and imagine pure white light flowing over and through it, dissolving any heaviness and restoring its natural, clear vibration.

BECKY – SHARING HEALING FROM THE HEART

Becky had been self-employed for many years when she first heard about a new US essential oil brand that had just arrived in the UK. From the moment she learned about it, something inside her lit up.

> *'It's hard to explain, I just knew. I knew they were powerful for healing before I'd even held them in my hands or smelled them. I knew I was meant to get the oils and share them with everyone.'*

She had a vision of these oils being in homes across the UK, supporting families in their everyday lives. Trusting her intuition, she waited for the right person to connect with. Eventually, she met her future mentor who sent her the oils from America and helped her run her first class. From there, Becky took the reins and began sharing the oils herself.

Today, she is regarded as one of the most respected essential oil specialists in the country. Her work not only gives her financial security for the rest of her life but also the freedom to spend time with her beloved family.

KEY TAKEAWAY: Becky is living her purpose by sharing her deep knowledge and love for something she believes is profoundly important. She inspires and motivates simply by sharing her passion and allowing it to ripple out to others.

THE ENERGY TOOL CATALOGUE

At the back of this book (see pages 186–7), you will find a catalogue of the best crystals and oils to use to enhance your Lightworker development, organized by theme and listed in the order in which you will tackle each topic.

That said, each soul has a unique lineage and experiences, which gives us all unique energy. This means that when using energy tools, we can't have a 'one size fits all' approach. For this reason, although I have included the crystals and essential oils that work well for most people, I always recommend trusting your intuition first, and work with the oil or crystal you are most drawn to in the moment. This will help your care routines become more personalized.

What Should I Heal First?

Now it's time to start identifying where you want to begin your healing journey. Other questions are going to arise as well, like how long you should keep working with a crystal or oil after you have done the initial Find Your Light Emotional Healing Protocol (see pages 80–1).

In the coming chapters, I'll introduce you to various intuitive skills but for now, so you can answer those questions, I'm going to show you one that anyone can do.

The Sway Test

When we use a pendulum, we are asking it for a yes or no answer. As we do this, our bodies strengthen in response to a positive answer. This is because we are firing up our primal 'fight' response, while a 'no' weakens the body, activating our 'flight' response.

The Sway Test takes away the pendulum and instead looks for the reactions in the body. When standing, our bodies move in one direction for a 'yes' and a different way for a 'no'. Usually, this is a sway back and forth, hence the name, but in reality, responses can have people go side to side, rotate or want to sit down.

I would suggest using the Sway Test to pick the first emotions you should focus on. Then you can use it to pick the right crystal or oil to use and pinpoint if you should be working with them after the initial healing and for how long.

THE SWAY TEST PROCESS

1. Have a drink of water so you know your muscles are hydrated.
2. Stand upright, feet hip-width apart. Keep your knees soft (not locked), arms at your sides and body relaxed.
3. With your eyes open, ask your body: What is my 'hard yes'? Stand quietly and observe how your body naturally responds. *Hint:* Asking for your 'hard yes' eliminates any uncertainty and creates a definitive answer.
4. Now ask: What is my 'hard no'? Again, observe your body and see what it does.
5. Now that you understand how your body indicates a 'yes' or 'no', you can start asking yes/no questions.

Light Code Activation: Find Your Light Emotional Healing Protocol

Now that we have explored the emotional and energy body – and how it's easier to initiate healing there rather than in the physical body – I will show you how to use crystals or essential oils as energy tools to release trapped emotions. This will allow you to heal those negative emotions of which you are already aware or that you pinpoint as you read the coming pages.

The aim is to turn the trapped energy (emotion) in the body into something tangible. Then, once we can imagine it, we can manipulate and change it. Remember: where you put your intention, change can happen.

THE FULL HEALING PROCESS

The full healing process, including preparation, is outlined below and opposite. Take your time to review each stage, source the crystals or essential oils you need and then wait for a moment.

Preparation

1. Use the Sway Test (see previous page) to identify which emotions need healing next.
2. Go to pages 186–7 to pinpoint the crystal or essential oil you should use.
3. Use the Sway Test once more to decide if you need any ongoing crystal or essential oil support and, if relevant, what that support should be.

Find Your Light Emotional Healing Activation

Now, with your crystal or essential oil to hand, bring to mind what you would like to focus on today.

1. Consider how the emotion or thought makes you feel. As you recall those memories, consider where in the body that feeling resides. Once you know, reach for your crystal or essential oil and do the following:
   - If you have a crystal, place it over the affected area.
   - If you have an essential oil, put one or two drops in the palms of your hands and inhale. Then, place the bottle over the area holding the emotion. *Hint:* If you cannot reach the area of the emotion, focus on the heart instead.
2. As you focus on the feeling, consider what 'colour(s)' it is. Focusing on that colour, imagine it changing to white. If it takes 5–15 minutes, that is normal, but if you feel the process is slowing down or stopping, take a moment to consider what colour the feeling is now. Then hold the intention that the new colour is changing to white.
3. Once the colour has almost disappeared, imagine it moving into the crystal or the essential oil bottle.
4. To disconnect from its energy, place the crystal or oil as far away as possible. Take a moment to rest before opening your eyes and having a glass of water.

PART 3

Healing and Reclaiming Your Power

'Set aside any preconceived notions about how the world views healing, and instead, hear these ancient insights with a fresh understanding.'

– THE AKASHIC RECORDS

CHAPTER 6

Healing the Past

'Remember, healing can be as simple as letting go of energy that shouldn't be there. Try and hold onto that thought so the job at hand does not overpower you.'

– THE AKASHIC RECORDS

It's Time to Look Back

Your perception of life is often filtered through past conditioning, which can cloud your decision-making and keep trapped emotions in place. These unresolved emotions can block the natural rise of your vibration, limiting your ability to fully step into your Lightworker potential. To resolve this, first we need to identify and heal what could be holding you back so that past pain does not slow or delay your Lightworker journey.

You don't need to pause your life to do this work – momentum matters – but it is important that you carve out some focused time to heal. You might devote a weekend to work through Part 3 all at once, or read through and choose your favourite techniques and fold them into to your daily routine (see pages 164–7).

We now know that Lightworkers use energy tools to support the energy body (see Chapter 5). Many of the methods are surprisingly simple; the harder part is identifying what actually needs to be healed.

In this chapter, we will address the emotions, fears, blocks and limiting beliefs that require your attention. We'll come to understand how emotions can build up in our energy field and learn practical methods to release them safely.

Law of Attraction

The Law of Attraction offers empowering lessons when we are exploring what needs healing. Consider this statement: *'You are a magnet, attracting everything in your life that you have brought to you energetically and you are currently repelling everything you want that hasn't yet manifested.'* In other words, your current vibration is matching your current reality. This reinforces how significant our frequency is to our reality.

When I first heard this idea, which was in the early stages of my spiritual development, I thought it sounded offensive. There were many things in my life that I wouldn't want to admit I had invited in. At the same time, I thought I was a 'good person' so why hadn't the nice things I'd hoped for materialized?

I now understand this statement is *far* from offensive – it's empowering! It highlights that life isn't happening to us; we have full autonomy to choose. In every moment, we are the total of every unhealed fear, block and belief. They are controlling us and creating our reality, even if it's a reality we don't want.

Understanding what changes we want by looking at what we are attracting into our lives is the starting point for healing. It is also a fast route to change because we don't have to find the root cause; instead, energy medicine focuses on the frequency of the issue, which reaches directly to the root cause.

JOURNALLING TIME

I invite you to find your favourite notebook and pen and create three titles:

- *What has manifested in my life that I want more of?*
- *What is in my life right now that I want to change or remove?*
- *What isn't in my life that I want to bring in?*

Now write down as many points as you can. Keep your journal close so that you can add more points as you think of them. After compiling this list for at least a day, ideally longer, look back and circle the three things that, if healed, would have the most significant impact for you and might help other areas of your life. These things – and any others you pinpoint when completing the journal prompts later in this chapter – are all emotions that the Find Your Light Emotional Healing Activation (see page 81) will help you to release.

Mirroring

When someone triggers us, whether through anger, jealousy, criticism or even admiration, it can be a sign that they are mirroring something we haven't entirely accepted, healed or integrated in our inner world.

For example, if someone's outspokenness deeply bothers us, it may point to an insecurity about expressing ourselves fully. Rather than focusing on changing or judging the other person, mirroring invites us to turn inward and explore why their behaviour affects us so strongly.

It's not about blame but about using emotional triggers as opportunities for self-awareness, healing and growth. Recognizing what we see in others often reflects what we need to see in ourselves.

As with the Law of Attraction, with Mirroring we don't need to start pinpointing the cause of each trigger, instead we can use the Find Your Light Emotional Healing Protocol (see pages 80–1) to release the energy around it so we can move on.

JOURNALLING TIME

1. On two separate pages of your journal, create the titles: *People* and *Events*.
2. Over a period of a few days, list people or events that have triggered strong negative emotions or reactions in you.
3. Now take the time to review your list and circle the three most emotive ones that if healed, might create the biggest outcome.

Negative Thought Patterns

Most of the time, long-term emotions and thought patterns manifest as fears, blocks or limiting beliefs. To understand these kind of thoughts, I'll outline what each of these is and give some examples of how you might experience them.

FEARS: Are emotional responses to perceived threats, real or imagined. They are often rooted in past trauma, subconscious beliefs, ancestral memory or societal conditioning. Fear is the brain's way of protecting you, but it can keep you from embracing life.

Examples of fear are: *Fear of failure, being alone, being seen, judgement, intimacy, success, rejection, abandonment, loss, not being in control, public speaking, speaking the truth, making a mistake, not belonging, failure and disappointing others.*

BLOCKS: Blocks often form due to trauma, repressed feelings, soul wounds or inherited patterns. Just like water that doesn't flow, the person's energy becomes murky and stagnant, which can lead to confusion, exhaustion, disconnection, resistance and a lack of motivation.

LIMITING BELIEFS: Subconscious thoughts or assumptions may restrict you from achieving your full potential. These beliefs often develop in childhood, through societal conditioning, trauma or repeated negative experiences. They can become the internal narrative that shapes your decisions, self-image and expectations of life.

Examples of limiting beliefs are:

- I'm not good enough
- I'm not worthy of love
- I'll never have enough money
- I'm too old to start over
- I'm not smart enough
- I'll be judged if I speak my truth
- It's not safe to be seen
- I'm not creative
- I always mess things up
- Nothing ever works out for me
- Love always leads to pain
- I'm not attractive enough
- People can't be trusted
- I'm bad with money
- I'm not intuitive
- My dreams are unrealistic
- I can't change
- I can't rely on anyone
- If I shine, people will leave me
- I must always please others
- I have to stay small to stay safe
- Good things don't last
- I'll always be alone
- I don't deserve happiness
- Life is a struggle
- I'm unlucky
- If I rest, I'm lazy
- I can't make a living doing what I love
- It's selfish to put myself first

JOURNALLING TIME

1. List any negative emotions you feel regularly and would like to overcome. You might want to go a step further and keep an emotions diary for a few weeks. Perhaps different emotions arise at different times of the month or during the different seasons (see page 58).
2. Now list any fears, blocks or limiting beliefs you are experiencing.
3. Once you have this list, circle the top three. Consider which ones, if healed, will help other areas of your life.

Healing Our Emotions

Emotions can be seen as 'energy in motion' so as they show up, they give us a good idea of the frequencies we are giving off and the themes and healings that need to take place. We need our energy to flow freely through each chakra. Any disruptions can show up as negative emotions or physical ailments. It is important we pinpoint the emotions we need to process, then as they heal, the energies lift and we can start to rebalance each chakra.

Below is a table showing the frequency and dimension that each emotion is in and the potential experience it might create. Interestingly, you can see how much higher the frequency a positive emotion is compared to a negative one. This shows how healing old thought patterns and choosing a positive mindset can dramatically shift our frequency and perception of the world.

3D to 5D Emotional Frequency Map

3D: EGO AND SEPARATION-FOCUSED: FREQUENCY: ROUGHLY 20–200HZ

LOW 3D: DENSE AND INWARDLY FOCUSED

- Hopelessness
- Grief and sorrow
- Feeling trapped
- Experiencing self-blame or shame
- Deep anger or hostility
- Envy
- Loss of motivation

MIDDLE 3D: REACTIVE

- Irritable and short-tempered
- Judging others
- Anxiety
- Uncertainty in self
- Sceptical
- Feeling overloaded

HIGH 3D: CONSTRUCTIVE BUT STILL SEEING THEMSELVES AS SEPARATE

- Restlessness
- Disinterested with a lack of drive
- A steady but neutral mood
- Tentative optimism

4D: AWAKENING AND EXPANDED AWARENESS: FREQUENCY: ROUGHLY 200–500HZ

LOW 4D: AWAKENING

- Questioning old beliefs
- Spiritually curious
- Yearning for deeper meaning
- Flashes of inspiration, followed by fear

MIDDLE 4D: CAN SEE THINGS CHANGING

- Clearer perspective on life events
- Awareness of habits and patterns
- Willingness to change
- Letting go of what drains their energy

HIGH 4D: LIVING FROM THE HEART

- Growing trust in intuition
- Feeling guided or supported
- Compassion for self and others
- Consistent sense of possibility

5D: HEART- AND SOUL-LED REALITY FREQUENCY: ROUGHLY 500–700HZ

LOW 5D: EXPLORING HIGHER STATES OF AWARENESS

- Positive outlook
- Trusting life
- Calm presence

MIDDLE 5D: EMPOWERED FLOW

- Strong faith in self and purpose
- Inner certainty
- Motivated
- Deep sense of purpose
- Daily gratitude
- Playful creativity

HIGH 5D: FULL ALIGNMENT

- Fulfilling their passions
- Blissful states
- Unconditional love
- Radiating joy

Here is a list of Energy Medicine modalities and the frequency scale they emit. As you can see, those frequencies are dramatically higher than those of the negative emotions they help overcome. When using these modalities, the higher frequencies pass through the body, releasing and taking the negative feelings away.

READINGS IN HZ

SOUND HEALING: Tuning forks, singing bowls and gongs: Range: <174 to 852Hz.

REIKI: There is no fixed Hz reading as the energy channelled depends on the practitioner's attention and the client's needs. However, Reiki is often likened to the love frequency, which is 528Hz.

READINGS IN MHZ

CRYSTAL HEALING: 70 to 120Mhz for grounding crystals; up to 300–400+Mhz for Ascension crystals.

ESSENTIAL OILS: Average 90–118Mhz, with rose reaching 320Mhz.

I have suggested various crystals and essential oils as your energy toolkit, which you can find in the Energy Tool Catalogue at the back of this book (see pages 186–7).

Forgiveness Work

Forgiveness work is the most powerful and important work of them all. People perceive forgiveness as allowing people who have wronged them to come back into their lives, but this isn't the case at all. Instead, it is about detaching from the past, not because they stop caring but so they can find happiness in the present.

As everything is energy, the kind of big events that require forgiveness work might have created an energetic cord between you and that event. Therefore, I see this work as being more about releasing them and that energy so we can move forward happier.

JOURNALLING TIME

1. Make a list of anyone you feel you need to do forgiveness work on. Try not to feel guilty if you need to add people close to you. Remember, this list is for your eyes only. We can care about someone and still need to add them.

Hint: I would also consider whether you need to add your own name. Often, we beat ourselves up over past decisions. In those cases, we need to forgive ourselves and our past actions.

Karma

Karma refers to the universal Law of Cause and Effect. Every action, thought or intention, good or bad, creates energy that will return to the individual in the future. At this point it will shape their experiences and life circumstances; it's about personal responsibility and the idea that *we reap what we sow.* The opposite of Karma is Dharma, which is the good we have done while alive. Our souls come here to learn lessons, no matter the journey chosen; the plan is to awaken, journey back to love via our predetermined purpose and reach Ascension.

INSTANT KARMA refers to a negative event that happens as a direct result of harmful behaviour we've engaged in during this lifetime. In this case, the Karmic debt is balanced within the same life.

DELAYED KARMA carries over into future lifetimes. It may appear as repeating patterns or unexplained challenges that seem to have no clear root cause, making them feel especially frustrating and challenging to resolve.

One of the reasons it is believed more souls and Soul Groups have incarnated now is so they can heal their Karma. This heavy energy weighs us down, hindering our move into the 5D. We might expect it to be hard to heal something rooted in a previous lifetime, when in fact it is easy. The answer is to live your Dharma through your Soul Purpose. Dharma is about living in harmony with our Highest Self and fulfilling our role in the world with integrity.

Over the years of teaching these theories, I have learned *that life is meant to be easy;* we humans make it hard. Acting out our Dharma heals our Karma because our purpose always involves acts of love, which we now understand come from a high frequency. As a result, our Karma cannot be held in a body, living at such a high frequency.

Your Karma will lift naturally as you journey towards your Soul Purpose, but to get you on that soul path, it is now necessary to focus on releasing the emotions and thought patterns you have journalled about.

Light Code Activation: Healing Across Time and Space

Having explored the trapped emotions that can be held in the body, this Activation will provide an Energy Healing to resolve as many of these emotions as possible.

Quantum Healing has helped us understand that we can only truly know we are healed when we acknowledge all dimensions and timelines where healing is needed. For that reason, all of these will be covered in this healing which will focus on our Soul Star Chakra because it is connected to our soul's energy and the part of us that has experienced all dimensions.

SOUL STAR QUANTUM HEALING

1. Once relaxed, start by becoming aware of your feet, then project your energies down to the Earth Star Chakra, roughly one metre (3ft) beneath you.
2. When you are ready, imagine white light coming up from this chakra and entering your feet. Let it travel through all areas of the body until it reaches the crown of your head.
3. While you focus on the breath, become aware of the Soul Star Chakra, roughly one metre (3ft) above your head. Imagine it as a magenta sphere.
4. Then imagine the white light at your crown travelling up and connecting to the Soul Star.

Soul Star Communication

5. Now, entirely focused on the Soul Star Chakra, on an inhale, slowly ask the question: *What colour are you in this lifetime?* Then, on the exhale, see what answer comes.

Although this chakra is usually magenta, if the answer is a different colour, this implies its energies have shifted and you need to do point 6, a Soul Star Healing. If the reply you receive is magenta, then you know on that level its energies are clear, and you can move to point 7.

SOUL STAR HEALING

6. Imagine the Soul Star as the colour that came through. Then take your time and slowly imagine that colour shifting to white light. Sometimes it will change to white immediately, while other times, it might have to transition through other colours first. Either way, all you need to do is focus on your breath and watch the colour(s) change until you reach white.

If at any point the process slows down or stops, ask the Soul Star what colour it is now. If a different colour comes, that is another layer of energy to release. If that happens, you simply follow the process again until that new colour has turned white. That is when you know all layers of healing have taken place.

Healing Across Time and Space

7. Once you have gone through and healed any layers that have built up in this life, you can start exploring other timelines. Ask your Soul Star: *Has your colour been affected by previous lives?* If it replies by showing magenta, it hasn't been affected and there is nothing to heal. If it replies with any other colour, you will need to go through the process outlined in point 6 again.
8. Once that is done, you can check the final two layers. *Is healing needed for any future lives? Is healing needed for lives in any other dimension or possibilities?*

Sealing the Activation

9. Once all healings have taken place, spend a moment sending gratitude to your Soul Star Chakra.
10. Then imagine white light travelling back down to the Crown Chakra.
11. Imagine any excess energy travelling down the body to the soles of your feet and releasing into the ground.

CHAPTER 7

Healing the Physical Body

'Your body is your greatest energy tool.'

– THE AKASHIC RECORDS

The Emotional Affects the Physical

Think about a time when you felt stressed before an important event and noticed your stomach tighten, or when worry kept you awake at night and left you exhausted the next day. These are examples of how emotions don't stay in the mind, they leave an imprint on the body. Until now, our focus has been on supporting the emotional body. In this chapter, we'll explore how that inner work also supports the physical body.

Energy medicine teaches that many physical ailments begin with an unresolved emotion or experience that weakens the energy body. This does not always come from a major trauma. Even something as ordinary as a minor fall can register in the body as more significant than it truly was, especially if the incident occurred when you were feeling stressed or tired.

When an area of the energy body becomes weakened, it is more likely to accumulate additional unprocessed emotions. Over time, these negative emotions build up until the energy becomes so dense it eventually starts manifesting as a physical ailment. Because the original cause is emotional, even when a challenge shows up in the physical body, the healing process still begins with releasing the underlying emotional root cause.

MEDICAL ADVICE

The practices, perspectives and tools shared in this chapter are intended for personal growth, self-reflection and energetic wellbeing. They are not a substitute for professional medical advice, diagnosis or treatment. Always consult with a qualified healthcare provider regarding any physical or mental health concerns. Never disregard or delay seeking medical advice because of something you have read in this book.

The Power of the Mind

Western medicine often focuses on managing symptoms, while holistic approaches look for the emotional root cause. Ancient healing methods can offer hope by reminding us that real change is possible, even in some of our most challenging moments.

Research shows that most of the body's cells regenerate within a year. This means that, in theory, and with the right support, nutrition and energy work, profound transformation is possible in a relatively short period of time.

We often hold beliefs about health and how best to heal. Many believe that Western medicine is the only path to healing. Others think that deep down, they don't deserve to be well. Some of us are out of touch with our inner power, not aware that it is possible to be a Healer, or that instant healing is possible.

The Double Split Experiment (see illustration below) taught us that we create our own reality. We have also explored how limiting beliefs can act as a barrier to us experiencing a different reality. Therefore if you notice resistance surrounding energy healing in yourself, I encourage you to explore any belief and where that belief comes from.

In Quantum Healing, this process is described as *collapsing timelines.* It asserts that there are multiple dimensions, and so it is possible for you to shift into a version of reality where healing has already occurred. Whether you see this as metaphor or multidimensional truth, the message remains the same: when the mind aligns with healing, the body often follows.

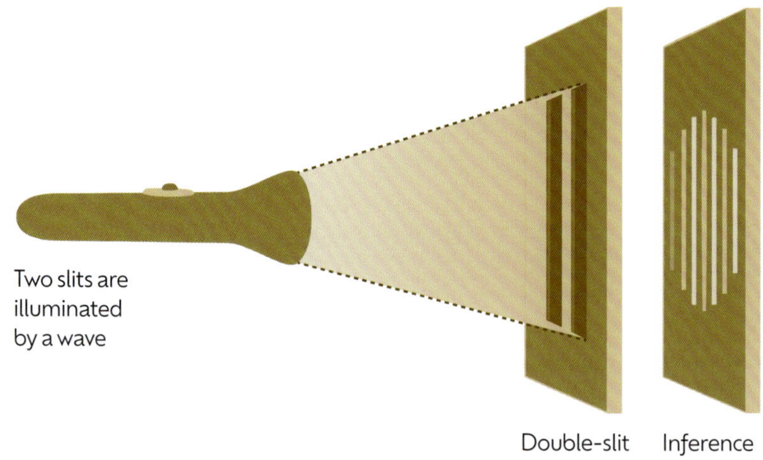

JENNIE – LISTENING TO THE QUIET KNOWING

When Jennie reflects on her life, one thread has always been constant: her deep trust in intuition. Years before a serious health challenge arose in 2016, she recalls feeling an unshakable inner knowing about the type of care and support she would choose for herself.

That summer, Jennie travelled to Cyprus for a holiday, packing a selection of essential oils 'just in case'. Within days, she was unexpectedly admitted to hospital for tests. During this time, she began using the oils, later discovering that each one supported her body's systems in ways that aligned with what she most needed at the time. Returning to the UK, further tests confirmed the nature and stage of her condition.

From that moment, Jennie embraced a holistic approach, incorporating daily essential oils, nourishing organic foods, targeted supplements and lifestyle changes that prioritized rest, nature and joy.

The Turning Point

Over the months that followed, Jennie's health shifted in ways that surprised even her. She describes this time as her *refining process.* A period in which she came to understand the depth of her connection to the natural world, the importance of listening to her body and the quiet wisdom of her own spirit.

JENNIE'S MESSAGE: *'Your body, your spirit and nature are in constant conversation. When you listen, you discover just how much guidance is already within you.'*

Light Code Activation: Find Your Light Physical Healing Protocol

Your body is always communicating with you – it provides clues, signals and messages that can guide your healing journey. The key is learning how to listen. Strengthening your intuition is crucial for this process, so if needed, visit Chapter 10 to learn how to reconnect with your body's wisdom. A simple daily practice, such as the Sway Test (see page 79), can also help you tune in and encourage your body to share what it needs.

In alignment with the Hermetic Principle of Cause and Effect (see page 61), every physical symptom has an underlying energetic or emotional root. Our physical health often mirrors our inner state, presenting as a metaphor for unresolved emotions or unprocessed experiences.

The table below highlights some areas of the body and the possible emotional patterns that may be contributing to ailments in those locations. This is not a rigid rule, but a guide to help you explore the emotional story behind your physical symptoms.

EMOTIONS BEHIND THE SYMPTOMS

ISSUE	POSSIBLE CONTRIBUTING FACTOR(S)
Back	Not feeling supported
Ears	Not liking something you heard
Eyes	Not liking something you saw
Heart	Issues with giving and/or receiving love
Knees	Fear of stepping into the future
Shoulders	Feeling the weight of the world on your shoulders

THE FULL HEALING PROCESS

On pages 80–1, I introduced you to an energy medicine protocol to support emotional healing. Now I will share an adaptation that supports the physical body. The process is similar, with just a small addition to help you identify the emotion behind any physical ailment. You will also need to imagine the feeling or emotion as a shape, rather than a colour, which represents its more physical form.

Preparation

1. Use the Sway Test (see page 79) to identify which physical ailment needs support.
2. Source either an Amethyst crystal or some Lavender essential oil.
3. Use the Sway Test to decide if you need any ongoing crystal or essential oil support and, if relevant, what that support should be.

Find Your Light Physical Healing Activation

Now, with your crystal or essential oil to hand, bring to mind what you would like to focus on today.

1. Consider how this physical ailment is affecting you and how it makes you feel emotionally (this is how we tap into the emotion behind the ailment). As you recall these emotions, consider where in the body that feeling resides. Once you know, reach for your crystal or essential oil and do the following:
   – If you have a crystal, place it over the affected area.
   – If you have an essential oil, put one or two drops in the palms of your hands and inhale. Then, place the bottle over the affected area. *Hint:* If you cannot reach the area of the emotion, focus on the heart instead. To acknowledge the underlying emotion involved, place your other hand over your heart.
2. As you focus on the feeling, consider what 'shape' it is. Focusing on that shape, imagine it getting smaller. If it takes 5–15 minutes, that is normal, but if you feel the process is slowing down or stopping, take a moment to consider what shape the feeling is now. Then hold the intention that the new shape is getting smaller.
3. Once the shape has almost disappeared, imagine it moving into the crystal or essential oil bottle.
4. To disconnect from its energy, place the crystal or oil as far away as possible. Take a moment to rest before opening your eyes and having a glass of water.

Light Code Activation: Quantum Healing Full Body Realignment

Now our emotional and physical healing is underway, this Activation embraces the concepts of Quantum Healing to help bring our physical health back into balance.

This visualization can take an hour. If you start to feel tired, you can do it in stages just as effectively. If at any point you feel resistance or self-doubt, make a note of what area of the body you had been focused on. Then work through that limiting belief before you focus on healing that area again.

QUANTUM HEALING TIMELINE VISUALIZATION

1. Set the intention: *I am now entering a Quantum Healing space.*
2. Start by imagining a bright gold healing light entering the Crown Chakra. Say out loud: *I am connecting to the highest timeline of healing.*
3. Imagine this light travelling through all areas of the brain and your nervous system. See your brain glowing with golden light. Picture all the neural pathways reorganizing, the inflamed or damaged areas disappearing. Affirm: *My mind is clear, focused and restored. I have shifted to full mental wellness.*
4. Now imagine your eyes becoming sharp and clear, like a lens adjusting perfectly; your ears attune to pure, perfect sound; your throat and vocal cords resonate with strength and clarity. Say: *I express truth. I perceive truth. I shift into perfect clarity and communication.*
5. Now bring your awareness down to your heart. Picture it glowing gold; every capillary pulses with fresh, clean, oxygen-rich blood. Affirm: *My heart is strong. I jump to the timeline of radiant circulation and emotional balance.*
6. See each lung expand with clean air. Say: *I breathe freely and deeply. I align with the timeline of complete vitality.*
7. Visualize the liver regenerating like a tree sprouting new leaves. Say: *My body detoxifies with ease. I leap to the timeline of total purification.*

8. Imagine your intestines unwind and light up gold. Affirm: *Digestion is smooth and peaceful.*
9. Picture the kidneys filtering with ease, the bladder releases toxins effortlessly. Any stones, inflammation or imbalances dissolve instantly. Affirm: *I release what no longer serves me. I cleanse and renew.*
10. Visualize your reproductive organs glowing with golden light, any trauma, pain or dysfunction is transmuted into vitality. Say: *I honour my creative life force. I leap to the timeline of healing and vitality.*
11. Imagine every bone aligning perfectly, your muscles relax and strengthen, your joints fluid and mobile. Affirm: *My structure is whole and strong. I step into my timeline of effortless movement and support.*
12. See your skin renewing in real-time, cells sparkling and refreshing. Say: *I radiate health from within. My skin reflects my highest healing timeline.*
13. See healing energy flowing down to your feet; any excess energy goes into the ground. Say: *I am grounded in wholeness. I stand firmly in my timeline of total wellness.* Visualize your entire body glowing with golden light.
14. Finish with this affirmation: *I choose this new reality. I am healed. I am whole.*

CHAPTER 8

Healing for the Future

'Watch the Universe and its Laws align for you.'

– THE AKASHIC RECORDS

Everything You Desire Can Be Yours

Whether your soul's focus is to pursue a particular career, embrace parenthood or finally prioritize a passion you've long set aside, this chapter is about moving forward with intention. Whereas previously we focused on healing the past to create space for new energy, now we turn toward the future.

When we explored the Law of Attraction (see page 86), the principle that like attracts like, we learned that what you hold in your thoughts, emotions and energy field determines what you draw toward you. But attraction alone is not enough. To live fully in flow, we must understand the Law of Manifestation, the process of directing energy so that what we envision can take form in the physical world. The ability to deliberately and intentionally manifest your desires is a natural and powerful gift for many Lightworkers.

At its core, manifestation is about energy flow. As you move through this book, you might notice certain opportunities, people or synchronicities have begun appearing almost effortlessly. This is the beginning of what's called *living in flow*, when living in alignment with your intuition and operating from a place of joy naturally magnetizes more of what you desire into your life. When you live in flow, you have truly achieved Ascension (see page 23) and 5D living (see pages 24–5).

By following the seven stages of the chakra manifestation process, you will identify where your flow may be blocked and learn how to bring each chakra into balance so that conscious manifesting becomes second nature.

The Law of Manifestation

'Everything is energy and that is all there is to it. Match the frequency of the reality you want and you cannot help but get that reality. It can be no other way. This is not philosophy. This is physics.' – ALBERT EINSTEIN

If we want to manifest positive change in our lives, it's best to do this consciously. Manifestation is closely connected to the Law of Attraction, which suggests that like a magnet, we attract what is in our life and repel what isn't. So, to welcome more of what lights us up, we need to shift our focus so it can enter.

The Line of Manifestation

In Chapter 3, we worked on opening and balancing the Line of Liberation, the upward flow of energy through the chakras from root to crown. Now, we'll focus on its counterpart, the Line of Manifestation, which flows downward from crown to root.

Just as before, emotions, events and situations from this life as well as previous lives can hinder this downward flow of energy. During the manifestation process, these blocks directly mirror the themes of each chakra stage. As we connect with each chakra, note the themes where you often feel blocked. By recognizing where your flow is restricted, you can begin to clear it, chakra by chakra, until living 'in the flow' becomes an effortless daily reality.

If at any point you are unsure whether you need to explore a certain chakra, perform the Sway Test (see page 79) or use a Pendulum (see pages 132–3). These tools can help you connect to your intuition so that what you need to heal comes to the surface.

Crown Chakra

The moments of inspiration that inspire new projects are received through the crown. These ideas and ah-ha moments are the first stage of manifestation. If you don't feel inspired or have been looking for inspiration but nothing comes, the Crown Chakra has likely closed.

This is common and nothing to worry about. The worrying events on the news are enough to close down this energy! The Crown Chakra does this to reduce the negative energies we are taking on; however, it then needs help to open up again.

When it is closed, it will hinder all the other chakras, so if moments of inspiration do not come easily to you, waking up this chakra could make all the difference.

Third Eye Chakra

If our Crown Chakra is open, we can receive regular insights and inspiration – this is why you might feel you get lots of new ideas. A balanced Third Eye will help you sift through the ideas, highlighting the best ones to move forward with. If that isn't happening and instead you are overwhelmed and have so many ideas that you're not sure how to progress, you need to balance your Third Eye – your intuitive insights and analytical skills can then help pinpoint the best ones. Again, make a note if this chakra needs support.

Throat Chakra

Once our Third Eye has identified the best ideas for you to consider, the energy moves into the Throat Chakra, where you can assess their feasibility. This begins with thoughtfully considering all aspects of the ideas, followed by sharing them with others.

At this stage, two things happen. You are either airing your ideas out loud, but there is still a good chance you won't go ahead with them, or you are subtly declaring to others that this *is* going to happen. The latter, our body interprets as a truth. Just like a 'yes' in the Sway Test, when we tell a truth, our body responds positively, and our heart can trust that it will happen, allowing the energies to move to the Heart Chakra.

When we are not speaking our truth but instead choose to air our ideas aloud, the Heart Chakra stays closed. You'll notice this if you often discuss ideas with people but rarely progress them.

Heart Chakra

When the energy of an idea falls into the Heart Chakra, we start to fall in love with it. That love and passion will drive the energy of the project. If you are in love with a project and start working towards making it happen, then you know the Heart Chakra's energy is balanced. However, if that love only lasted for a short time and you never actually started to progress things further, then your Heart Chakra needs extra support.

This can happen when we have had a lot of setbacks in life, misfortune or heartbreaks. Bringing that chakra back into balance will aid in healing those old wounds and allow you to fully embrace anything that you are passionate about.

Solar Plexus Chakra

The start of a new project can feel clumsy, especially as we prepare to bring everything together, but as long as you begin and there is clear direction, then your solar plexus is in balance and working well.

In contrast, if you are someone who suffers from procrastination, regularly delaying a new project, perhaps due to a lack of energy or prioritizing other jobs first, then your solar plexus needs support. Imposter syndrome is a classic sign that your solar plexus needs more energy. This chakra is the home of our ego, so imbalances happen here when there is a lack of confidence. Even overconfidence can create problems, as we might then fear doing something new, since it might not show us at our best. If this resonates with you, it is important to focus on balancing your solar plexus.

Sacral Chakra

When we settle into a new project, our energies will move into the Sacral Chakra, where they will stay until it ends. If it is a large project, we can remain in Sacral Chakra energy for a long time so a lot of willpower, a trait of this chakra, is needed.

You will know this energy is out of balance if you start a lot of projects but don't finish them.

Root Chakra

When you have completed your goal, that is when your energies fall into the Root Chakra. This chakra is the most dense in frequency, so it represents the physical world and what you have created or achieved.

If you have a balanced Root Chakra, you will happily celebrate your achievement with your friends and family. However, an out-of-balance chakra manifests as difficulty telling others about your creations. Examples of this might include an artist who doesn't want to display their artwork, a person who doesn't celebrate milestones or a child who fears sharing the song they've learned to play. Balancing the Root Chakra will help those people feel and show pride in their achievements.

Time to Heal

At this point, you have made a list of chakras and specific issues that need support. If more than three chakras are listed, I would suggest focusing on the three positioned higher on the body. These will be a higher vibration than the others, so that change will happen quicker. Once healed, they might even heal the ones underneath them. To balance the chakras, use the Emotional Healing Activation on page 81. This time, using the relevant chakra crystals and oils you will find on pages 186–7. Once you have worked on those three, allow two weeks for the energies to shift and settle, then use the Sway Test (see page 79) or a Pendulum (see pages 132–3) to ask if any other chakras need to be balanced to improve your manifestation skills.

Sacral Chakra: Aragonite

Root Chakra: Garnet

Sacral Chakra: Yellow Calcite

Throat Chakra: Blue Lace Agate

Heart Chakra: Green Aventurine

Third Eye Chakra: Purple Fluorite

Crown Chakra: Howlite

NICOLA – FINDING SOUL PURPOSE UNEXPECTEDLY

Nicola works in a position that carries a level of responsibility most people would shy away from. On the surface, it may seem far removed from the heart-led settings we often associate with spiritual fulfilment, but Nicola knows she was guided there.

Following the Red Thread

Nicola can see a Red Thread running through her career, each role leading seamlessly to the next. Years ago, she saw her current position on TV and felt a spark of recognition: *'I would love to do that one day.'* At the time there was no clear route, yet the Universe played its part. Two promotions later, she found herself in the exact role she had admired from afar.

It's a reminder that you don't always need to know *how* something will happen, only that it's meant for you.

Purpose in an Unlikely Environment

Given that Nicola's personality is almost the opposite of many of her colleagues, I asked how she feels aligned with her purpose in such a contrasting environment. Her answer was simple: 'I know my purpose is to be the grounding light in the room.' Her contribution isn't just about tasks; it's about the energy she brings, helping to steady discussions and bring balance when situations threaten to spiral.

Nicola admits that navigating strong personalities can be challenging. She applies the concept of *mirroring*, reflecting at the end of each day:

- *Who challenged me today?*
- *Who mirrored something back to me?*
- *What lesson did I learn from it?*

This practice and level of awareness keep her grounded and turn difficult encounters into growth.

KEY TAKEAWAY: Your Soul Purpose isn't tied to a specific job or environment. Sometimes, your role is to bring light and awareness into places that might otherwise lack it.

Light Code Activation: Quantum Manifesting

Now you understand just what is happening when you manifest, it is time to embrace all your learnings and use a process called Quantum Leaping to step into the version of you that has already achieved your dream.

Being clear about what you want is part of the process. For that reason, we are about to embark on a technique to help you step onto the timeline where you already know what your future path is. From there the knowledge, lessons and insights you need to make this change will come to you faster, so by the time we reach Part 4 you are already receiving guidance and moments of inspiration helping lead you towards this path.

WHAT IS QUANTUM LEAPING?

Many believe that every time we make a decision, there is an aspect of us, in a different dimension, that chooses the alternate route. Once we have this awareness, we can choose to jump onto the timeline that has everything we already want. For this to be possible, our energies must be instantly aligned with that goal, so we can bring it into our reality much faster.

QUANTUM LEAP YOUR MANIFESTATION

1. Standing up, close your eyes and take the time to recall the dream life you have journalled about. Remember all the small details so it's as vivid as possible.
2. Now consider how that life will make you feel? This helps you tap into its energy.
3. Imagine a version of yourself in front of you that is living that life. Consider if they are like you? If something is different, what is it?
4. Now, with complete joy, shout 'I choose my dream life'. Then jump so you are standing in the place of that dream aspect of you – and celebrate your Quantum Leap!

CHAPTER 9

Shadow Work for Lightworkers

'Healing has layers but that shouldn't hold you back. Do the work and do what you love at the same time. Remember the Universe loves duality, so embrace it. Be in the dark for a moment so the light is even brighter.'

– THE AKASHIC RECORDS

Healing isn't Linear

You are now well on your way to clearing trapped emotions and embracing your Light. Yet, when it comes to healing, the process is certainly not linear. As you move forward, it is essential to pause regularly, reflect and revisit layers of insights, emotions and healing that continue to emerge.

Your expanding awareness and developing 5D perspective mean you now understand how to shift energies to dissolve old patterns. However, you will find that as you do so, deeper layers of emotion – personal, generational or even past-life traumas – will become unearthed.

Shadow Work is a key part of your ongoing journey. It is the practice of uncovering these unprocessed or unconscious aspects of ourselves – our Shadow – and transforming them into light. You can only truly experience the Light by acknowledging and integrating the Dark. Continuous Shadow Work will ensure any hidden inherited emotions that arise are properly addressed so that you can continue moving forward towards your highest potential.

What is Shadow Work?

Shadow Work can be broken down into five broad categories:

1. SOCIALLY UNACCEPTABLE BEHAVIOURS: Patterns or actions we might hide from others or ourselves out of fear of judgement.
2. HIDDEN EMOTIONS: Repressed feelings that linger beneath any conscious awareness.
3. SOUL-INHERITED TRAUMA: Energies and experiences carried over from past lifetimes.
4. ANCESTRAL TRAUMA: Emotional imprints passed down through your lineage.
5. LIGHTWORKER SPECIFIC SHADOWS: Unique blocks or challenges tied to your purpose and heightened sensitivity.

These Shadow Energies often manifest as dense emotions that sit at the very bottom of the 3D to 5D Emotional Frequency Map (see pages 90–1). Many may not appear in your healing lists because they so deeply hidden, especially past-life and inherited energies. As you raise your vibration, these heavier energies become noticeable, and three things may happen:

1. Forgotten or buried memories resurface.
2. Lingering sadness or heaviness appears despite recent joyful breakthroughs on your Lightworker journeys.
3. Your intuition signals it's time to address a specific theme, sometimes clearly, sometimes through repeated signs or synchronicities.

To work through these energies, use tools such as the Sway Test (see page 79) or a Pendulum (see pages 132–3) to identify the areas that need your attention. Once a pattern or issue is discovered, return to the Find Your Light Emotional Healing Protocol (see pages 80–1) to process and integrate this shadow energy fully.

Socially Unacceptable Behaviour

One of the key lessons in Shadow Work is embracing the idea that all humans are capable of all emotions and behaviours. The difference is that we *choose* not to act on the more dangerous or socially unacceptable ones, and we hide those away in what's known as our Shadow Self.

However, our upbringing and society often condition us to suppress not only harmful behaviours, but also powerful and positive aspects of ourselves. For example, if someone is taught not to appear 'too confident', they may suppress a natural leadership quality, which, if embraced, could help them thrive.

This kind of Shadow Work also often includes healing around social and gender-based conditioning. A classic example is the belief that women should be pleasing, softly spoken and non-confrontational. This can prevent someone from speaking up when they need to or from expressing anger in healthy ways. Using your voice to set boundaries or express hurt is a completely justified and empowering response.

Shadow Work can also deal with the pressure many of us feel to conform. For example, following a traditional life path simply because it was expected of us, when deep down, our soul longed for something different. That's why so many Lightworkers find themselves facing Shadow Work. Wanting to follow their soul's unique path often brings up old fears and programming. It's through facing these shadows that we reclaim our truth, our power and our light.

MY SHADOW WORK STORY

As a child I was often told 'children should be seen and not heard.' As a result, I developed a shy, quiet personality. As I began to step into my Soul Purpose and intuitively sensed that it would involve teaching and public speaking, those old beliefs surfaced. In the early days of teaching, I would lose my voice every time I led a class. My Throat Chakra was so underactive that even a small amount of teaching completely depleted it. It wasn't until I began using the Shadow Work techniques in this book that those symptoms disappeared. Today, I speak regularly without any of those issues.

Hidden Emotions

A common form of Shadow Work that many of us need to overcome is the healing of dense emotions we can experience, including guilt, shame, regret, resentment, hate, anger and jealousy. You might have already done some work around these emotions. Even so, I would ask your body if there is still anything there that needs healing.

Soul-Inherited Shadows

The reason Shadow Work can at times be so hard to unravel is that it can include trauma that our souls experienced in a previous life that had such an impact, it is still playing out today. These traumas can include phantom pains which originate from life-threatening wounds inflicted in a past life or a reluctance to speak out now because you were attacked for those same opinions in a previous life.

Ancestral Trauma

We can also inherit Shadow Work from our Ancestors. Many Lightworkers are here to heal the long-standing trauma and Karma that is stopping them and their families from raising their vibration (see page 95).

Ancestral Healing refers to the process of addressing unresolved trauma, beliefs, patterns and Karma inherited from one's lineage. These imprints can affect our emotional, psychological, physical and spiritual wellbeing. The table opposite details different ancestral wounds or soul imbalances that may need healing.

TRAUMA	EXPLANATION	EXAMPLES
GENERATIONAL TRAUMA	Trauma experienced by ancestors (war, genocide, abuse, slavery, displacement) that is passed down through genetics, family patterns or energetic memory.	A descendant might carry anxiety or hypervigilance due to an ancestor's experience in a war zone.
CULTURAL OR ETHNIC DISCONNECTION	Loss of connection to one's cultural roots, traditions, language and rituals due to colonization, migration or assimilation.	Feeling spiritually unmoored or out of place due to a lack of connection with one's heritage.
UNACKNOWLEDGED ANCESTORS	Ancestors who were forgotten, dishonoured, or excluded.	Recurring family dysfunction is tied to an ancestor who died under tragic or secretive circumstances.
ANCESTRAL GUILT OR SHAME	Inherited feelings of guilt or shame due to ancestors' harmful actions (participation in slavery, violence, betrayal).	Descendants might carry subconscious self-sabotage or unworthiness.
PATRIARCHAL OR MATRIARCHAL WOUNDS	Dysfunctional patterns in the masculine or feminine lineage (suppression of women, toxic masculinity, wounded fatherhood).	Difficulty with authority, gender identity or relationships due to unhealed parental lineage wounds.
SPIRITUAL OR RELIGIOUS TRAUMA	Pain passed down from forced conversions, witch hunts, religious persecution or misuse of spiritual authority.	Fear of spiritual power or distrust in spiritual institutions.
VOWS, CONTRACTS AND CURSES	Energetic imprints from ancestral vows (poverty, silence, celibacy) or curses placed intentionally or unintentionally across generations.	Repeated financial struggles due to an ancestral vow of poverty taken by a monk/nun.
LOSS OF LAND AND DISPLACEMENT	Trauma from forced removal from land, colonization, displacement or migration.	A soul-level sense of not belonging, rootlessness or deep grief tied to homeland loss.
UNFINISHED BUSINESS OR UNRESOLVED GRIEF	Emotional burdens from ancestors who died suddenly, or with regret or unfulfilled dreams.	A descendant may feel inexplicable grief or a desire to 'complete' something left unfinished.
INHERITED BELIEFS AND PATTERNS	Limiting beliefs or coping mechanisms inherited from family, often unconsciously.	'We don't trust outsiders' or 'Money is evil' shape life choices and behaviours.
ADDICTION AND MENTAL HEALTH LEGACIES	Patterns of addiction, depression or other mental health issues passed down as coping mechanisms or unresolved pain.	Multiple generations are suffering from alcoholism or mood disorders.
ABUSE AND VICTIM-PERPETRATOR DYNAMICS	Cycles of abuse that repeat across generations without healing or accountability.	Abusers and victims are showing up in different roles across generations.
SUPPRESSED GIFTS AND WISDOM	Spiritual or creative gifts that were hidden or denied due to persecution or fear.	Healers or seers in the lineage whose talents were feared or condemned, leading descendants to fear their own intuition.

Quantum Healing in Action

You can see that Ancestral Work is complex and varied, but you know you don't have to relive the trauma before you can heal. If you are drawn to learn more, you can use the Higher Heart Spirit Team Meeting Activation (see pages 160–1) to bring in your Ancestors and understand what they went through. These insights can help the healing go deeper.

The magic of Ancestral Healing is that what we heal today also heals our Ancestors. So, although this work is deep and complex, healing their trauma and Karma is a gift we can pay back to those who came before us.

Lightworker's Shadows

We know as Lightworkers that being here now is essential, but it is sometimes alright to wish you were 'normal' and just 'fitted in'. Here are some of the emotions and situations Lightworkers regularly encounter:

- Learning to be okay with being 'different' and having 'different' interests.
- Being okay with the family or community member who doesn't like you choosing a different path.
- Learning to be confident speaking on Lightworker topics.

Light Code Activation: Transmuting Energies with the Violet Flame

It's time to teach you the 5D healing practice of the Violet Flame. This is a divine energy of purification, transformation and forgiveness. When we invoke it, we are calling on a high-frequency light that can cleanse negative energy and clear Karma, making this the perfect healing process for Shadow Work.

St Germain is an Ascended Master known for his wisdom, alchemy and spiritual transformation. Often called the *Keeper of the Violet Flame*, he is believed to have gifted humanity this healing tool to transmute lower energies into higher frequencies. That's why St Germain is often called upon during Violet Flame visualizations and healing practices.

Transmuting Energy with the Violet Flame

1. Once relaxed, take a few deep breaths and clearly state your intention, either silently or out loud: *I call on the Violet Flame to help me transmute … into light, love and healing.*
2. Then invite in the Violet Flame by saying: *With the divine guidance of St Germain, I invite in the Violet Flame.*
3. Imagine a swirling violet flame in your heart. It expands and surrounds you.
4. Now, recall the Shadow Work you would like to transmute. Say inwardly, *I acknowledge this feeling and now I choose to let it go.*
5. Visualize the emotion as a shape, colour or energy in your hands.
6. Gently offer it into the Violet Flame.
7. Watch it dissolve, transmute and rise like smoke.
8. Now, imagine the Violet Flame changing colour slightly, becoming a brilliant lavender-gold light. Feel this light entering your heart, filling it and any other places once affected by that energy.
9. Now decree what you want that energy to become. Pick an emotion you need, for example: peace, strength or compassion.
10. Thank the Violet Flame and St Germain.
11. See the flame reduce in size and return to the heart.

PART 4

Embodying Your Light

'This is when you see everything differently!'

– THE AKASHIC RECORDS

CHAPTER 10

Trusting Your Light

'Listen to the whispers of the world. Just as regular as birds singing in the dawn chorus, trust that you are guided all day, every day. Distrust is a human condition; trust is the soul's natural state.'

– THE AKASHIC RECORDS

The Power of Intuition

By now, your healing process is well under way, and you are ready to step firmly into the next stage of your Lightworker path. From here, growth comes not only from clearing the past but from aligning with your future. This chapter is about helping you move even closer to your 5D lifestyle through three energy upgrades: learning to access your intuitive skills, discovering your Soul Purpose and beginning to live a Lightworker lifestyle.

The foundation for all of these upgrades is intuition. Your intuition is your most powerful guide – more powerful than any outside source including friends, family or even professionals! While guidance from our loved ones is invaluable and well-meaning, it comes filtered through their own lived experiences and beliefs, and may not be the best option for you.

In contrast, intuition comes directly from your Higher Self, the wisest part of you that knows your soul's plan for this lifetime. From this place, intuition offers insights perfectly tailored to you. It helps you navigate choices and recognize opportunities that are aligned with your Soul Purpose. In a world filled with noise and misinformation, learning to listen to your inner guidance ensures you stay rooted in your authentic truth. This is the first step toward living fully in your Light.

What is My Intuition?

Intuitive messages come from two primary sources. The first comes from the subconscious mind, which is always scanning our environment to keep us safe. This is the classic fight-or-flight mechanism, often experienced as a gut-level *yes – no*, sometimes accompanied by an internal voice or dialogue. Simple techniques such as the Sway Test (see page 79) help us access and interpret this type of guidance.

The second source comes from the Soul Star Chakra, flowing into our awareness through the Third Eye. These messages carry a higher level of wisdom. Instead of simple signals, they often arrive as deep insights, detailed thoughts or even visual clues that point us toward our soul's bigger purpose.

How are Psychic Skills Different from Intuitive Guidance?

While intuition connects us with our own inner wisdom and Higher Self, psychic skills go a step further by accessing energies and information from beyond ourselves. In essence, psychics tap into energies separate from themselves, such as the superconscious (see page 56), spirit guides (see pages 155–6) or other energetic realms such as the Akashic Records (see page 15). Examples of psychic abilities include:

- Mediumship – connecting with ancestors and spirits
- Telepathy – sensing the thoughts or emotions of others
- Downloads – receiving messages from higher beings

At the core, it is all energy. Intuition tunes us inward, while psychic skills tune us outward to different, external energetic sources. And while this skill may feel out of reach right now, many people – especially Lightworkers – discover these abilities naturally once they begin working with their energy.

We will put your psychic development to practice in Chapter 12 when you meet your Spirit Team, but for now, focus on strengthening your intuitive guidance – the foundation for everything that follows.

Banishing Self-Doubt

As a child psychic, I have had conversations about intuition for as long as I can remember. One thing I've noticed is that most people confidently declare *'I'm not intuitive.'* Why do so many people doubt themselves?

Part of the problem is how intuition and psychic abilities are portrayed in media. Films depict dramatic visions of people seeing spirits in the real world, predicting the future in vivid detail or reading minds like a superheroes. While exciting on screen, this exaggerated imagery can cause us to overlook the more subtle ways our intuition communicates with us.

EMMA – BLENDING LOGIC AND MAGIC

When Emma first began exploring the holistic world, she stood on the sidelines. She quietly observed the energy radiating from spiritual groups like mine. Eventually, curiosity drew her in and she kept returning, drawn by the inspiration and sense of belonging.

From Crystals to a Calling

Emma's journey began long before she recognized it. As a child, she was drawn to crystals. A quiet passion that resurfaced just as she began questioning her direction.

At first, she focused on weight loss, believing it would unlock her happiness. She did exceptionally well, reaching her goal weight, but the emotional fulfilment she expected never came. This was her crossroads.

She returned to her love of crystals and explored many healing techniques until she found the ones that resonated most deeply.

A Unique Perspective

Emma proudly identifies as an Earthseed, deeply connected to Mother Nature and the physical world, knowing she's lived many lifetimes here. Through her new business, *All About Holistics*, she helps other left-brained people explore different healing modalities.

As a process-loving person, she describes herself as 'Mindfully Mindful', scheduling daily spiritual practices and using crystals, oracle cards and energy work as tangible tools for everyday life.

EMMA'S MESSAGE: Try different things until you find what lights you up. Even if the first step doesn't resonate, keep going. The path will lead somewhere profound.

KEY TAKEAWAY: You don't have to abandon logic to embrace your spiritual gifts. Emma knows that blend is where her purpose thrives.

Pendulums and Oracle Cards

Using pendulums and oracle cards is a good way for us to start developing our intuition because they help us to produce the messages, taking the pressure off us.

Pendulums as Energy Tools

Pendulums are a great way to tap into your inner knowing and intuition with swift 'yes' or 'no' questions (see page 79). Working with a pendulum involves holding a pendulum or weighted necklace at chest height, asking questions and paying attention to the pendulum's movement to indicate a 'yes' or 'no' response. Like the Sway Test (see page 79), pendulums work because our bodies strengthen in response to a positive answer, swinging the pendulum in a particular direction. This is because we are firing up our primal 'fight' response, while a 'no' weakens the body, activating our 'flight' response.

USING A PENDULUM

1. With the pendulum relaxed (not swaying), ask the following in your head or out loud: *What is my hard yes?* Then the pendulum might do a number of different things, from swaying in a specific direction, rotating or wobbling.
2. Watch the pendulum make the same movement several times. This is your 'yes'.
3. Now ask for your 'hard no'. *Hint:* The movement won't necessarily be the opposite of your 'yes'.
4. Once you know your 'hard yes' and 'no', you can start asking questions.

PENDULUM TIPS

Always ask to see your hard yes and hard no each time, as this can change. If you are not getting a reaction, it's likely you're dehydrated, which means your muscles aren't firing correctly. Drink some water and then try again.

Oracle Cards

Once your intuition can offer 'yes' and 'no' answers, the next stage is to receive more in-depth responses. Oracle Cards are a good first step towards receiving longer intuitive messages. These are decks of cards depicting images and text relating to a specific theme.

PICKING YOUR IDEAL ORACLE DECK

There are numerous decks available, depicting every theme you can imagine. Always pick the deck you're drawn to. That is your intuition indicating that it has the messages you need. When you are drawn to a different deck, that new deck has the right messages.

How to Use Oracle Cards

1. Think of the question you would like answered. You might want to start by picking a card which offers 'general guidance'.
2. With a clear mind, start shuffling the cards. This familiarizes you with their size while you start to unconsciously pick up on the subtle frequency of the messages and images on each card.
3. Still shuffling, in your mind's eye, think of your question. As you do this, your energy field becomes that question and you will be attracted to the card with the right message.
4. Now, shuffle the cards and pick one.
5. Translate the meaning of that card in relation to your question.
6. If the card's message isn't clear, you might need to draw a second card to receive the whole message.

How to Translate the Meaning of a Card

There are two ways to interpret the message on a card:

THE MEANINGS BOOK: All decks come with a book, which offers the author's meaning for each card.

INTUITIVELY TRANSLATE THE CARD: This means picking a card, looking at it and seeing what the image and any text mean to you. At any given moment, we only take in 20 per cent of what we are looking at, so each time you take a card, you will see something different. What you see will be relevant to your current reading. In a future reading, you will only see what is relevant to that reading. As everything is energy, you are drawn to the messages that answer your current question.

Hint: Our intuition likes to work in metaphors so understanding symbolism is important. A card depicting a tree might refer to the tree in your garden, but it might also mean your family tree or making roots for yourself. Always trust that what you think of in the moment is the right translation for that reading.

Internal Guidance

Once you have perfected both intuition tools, I recommend starting to explore how your intuition can offer you direct guidance. This involves receiving messages directly from the body via your Clair Senses.

Clair Senses are intuitive abilities that correspond to our physical senses but operate on an energetic level. Each Clair Sense connects to a particular part of the body and can be experienced in subtle, personal ways.

It is important to note that most people don't have all the Clairs. Normally, as we open up to this work, we start with one or two. Then as you learn to trust your intuition, more skills become available to you. Some we use daily, while others we might experience once or twice in our lives.

Clair Senses

CLAIRVOYANCE (CLEAR SEEING)

The ability to receive intuitive information through images, visions, colours or symbols. How you might experience this Clair:

- Seeing internally, with your Third Eye: Seeing visuals, memories, colours or symbols while your eyes are closed.
- Seeing messages in the world around you: Asking an intuitive question, then glancing at something that symbolically has the answer. Noticing the same thing more than once in a day.

CLAIRAUDIENCE (CLEAR HEARING)

The ability to receive intuitive information through audio messages or sound in the Third Eye or the world around us. How you might experience this Clair:

- Hearing internally with your Third Eye: Songs, audio or an inner voice which might sound like you or someone else. Ringing in the ears.
- Hearing messages in the world around you: Hearing a name, word, song lyric or advice out of the blue.

CLAIRCOGNIZANCE (CLEAR KNOWING)

Instantly knowing something without logical reasoning. How you might experience this Clair:

- If you need to choose between several options, Claircognizance will highlight the right ones so strongly that you won't be able to pick a different option. You just *know* it's the right thing to do.

CLAIRSENTIENCE (CLEAR FEELING)

The body uses emotions or physical sensations as a message. How you might experience this Clair:

- Sudden mood changes without a clear source.
- Gut feelings or physical sensations like tightness, tingling or chills.

Clairsentience becomes an empathic skill when you start picking up emotions and sensations that someone else is feeling. This skill is often called Clairempathy. Being an 'Empath' is a common Lightworker trait.

CLAIRTANGENCY (CLEAR TOUCH)

Receiving information by physically touching objects or people (also called psychometry). This skill is particularly strong in Healers. How you might experience this Clair:

- Holding an object allows you to see its history or owner.
- Touching someone, you might sense their emotional or physical state.

CLAIRALIENCE (CLEAR SMELLING) AND CLAIRGUSTANCE (CLEAR TASTING)

Smelling scents that are not coming from something physically present and tasting something without actually eating or drinking it. Both Clairalience and Clairgustance can be a way to recall memories. As a psychic skill, they are often linked to spirit communication or memories.

Some Clair messages are particularly hard to translate, especially if your intuition communicates in colours, emotional or physical sensations. If you receive messages like this, I suggest asking your oracle cards what they mean. Once you understand the message, normally it is the same translation each time.

How to Connect to Your Inner Guidance

Now that we understand how our intuition can communicate, we can try and receive some messages. You need to find somewhere quiet, where you won't be disturbed, so you can do the following:

1. Sit in a relaxed position, eyes closed. Focus on the breath for a few moments.
2. Start to lengthen the breath. If your natural breath count is three or four, try extending it to four or five, and then aim for five or six. Make sure the exhale is as slow as the inhale.
3. On a very slow inhale, ask a question. Here are some suggested questions to start with:
   - *What do I need to know right now?*
   - *What emotion do I need to heal next?*
   - *What small step can I take today to feel more loved?*
   - *What do I need to do to raise my vibration?*
4. On an equally slow exhale, open up all your senses and see what message comes through.
5. If a message does not come right away, ask again. It can take a few attempts to get a response.

Remember, the body can reply with any Clair sense even if you ask a question and then find yourself opening your eyes and looking at something, that will be the message. The golden rule is, *Everything that happens when you're connecting to your intuition can be a message!*

Perfecting your Intuitive Skills

When we first start actively connecting to our Clair senses, there is a lot to perfect; it can take some time for messages to come.

If you are having trouble connecting normally, it may be because you are not relaxed enough. In our waking state, we are in a Beta Brainwave state. However, these days we spend a lot more time in High Beta, which is a fight or flight (stress) state. To connect to our intuition easily, we need to relax into a Theta brainwave state, which is the equivalent of being in a light sleep.

In other words, when we are stressed, we are not aligned with that energy, so we need to relax more. Even when relaxed, you might struggle to pick up intuitive messages. In those cases, just like the pendulum, I would ask your intuition to amplify the messages so that they are easier to pick up.

BRAINWAVE STATES

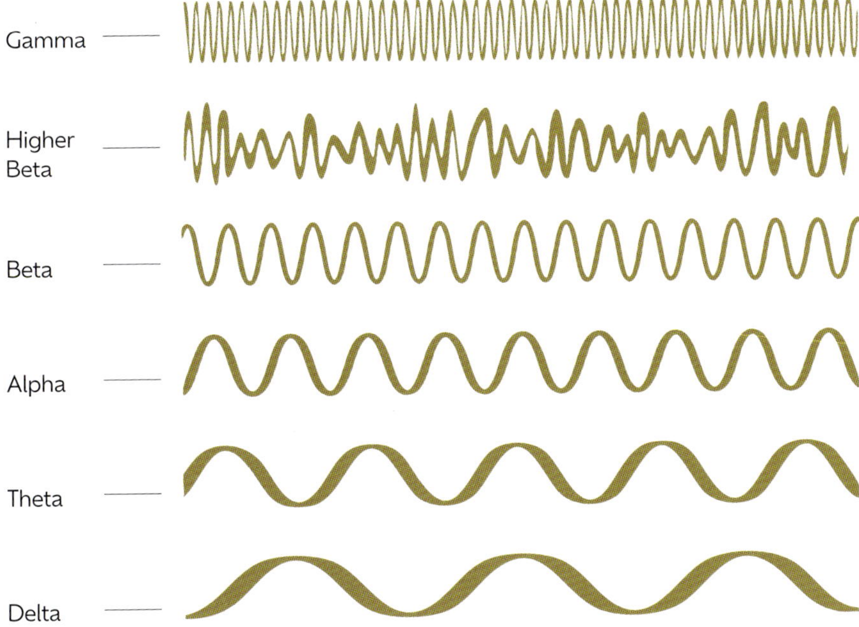

Secondary Questions

Typically, we tend to ask our intuition a question, receive the response and then move onto the next question. An easy way to progress your intuitive skills is to take a moment to consider the answers, then ask more questions when needed; I call these *Secondary Questions.* Consider if you need to seek more clarity. Alternatively, can you go deeper and ask for more context or insight on how you can progress their suggestions.

Building Trust

Once you are receiving messages, the next stage is learning to trust that those messages are from your intuition, as opposed to just normal thoughts. Thoughts created by the ego feel like a lengthy, stressful dialogue. In contrast, our intuition is highly succinct. It can answer a whole question in just three words and the message will feel calm and relaxed. When unsure, consider how the message was delivered.

In the beginning, you might find that guidance comes as small daily tasks which, if completed, lead towards your bigger goals. This is deliberate because your Higher Self knows you are learning to trust it, so it gives you small, easy-to-follow steps, allowing you to receive confirmation that it works.

We are all intuitive and it's a powerful tool. We just need the space to understand it, trust it and perfect it. Seek guidance if you experience self-doubt; don't let it get in the way of a gift that will support you for the rest of your life.

Light Code Activation: Activating Your Higher Chakras

Now that you are embodying the Lightworker lifestyle, it's time to activate your Higher Chakras, which will heighten your Lightworker skills, particularly your intuition. Do this before bed so the awakened chakras integrate as you sleep.

Higher Chakra Activation

1. Once relaxed, bring your awareness to the Earth Star Chakra beneath your feet. Imagine you are drawing white light up into your feet, then up through the body, all the way to the Crown Chakra. View that white light travel up to your Soul Star Chakra, then up to your Stellar Gateway.
2. From this point, you are going on a journey back down the body, connecting to specific areas and waking up the chakra energies.
3. Imagine a white chakra at the back of your head. This is your Causal Chakra. Once activated, it allows your Third Eye to receive higher frequency channelled messages. Keep your focus on that chakra until you see its energy growing bright. Then carry on down the body, focusing on each of these areas, waiting until their energies feel fully open and expansive, before moving onto the next chakra:
    - **Past Life Chakra:** A pale violet light behind the ears, it helps us remember what we did before this life.
    - **Akashic Records Chakra:** A rainbow ray at the back of the neck, it connects us to the Akashic Records.
    - **Higher Heart Chakra:** Turquoise light over the thymus, this connects the Heart and Throat Chakras, teaching us the higher lesson of speaking with compassion and empathy.
    - **Inner Sun:** A gold disc over the solar plexus, enables us to be our true selves, free of fear of others' perceptions.
    - **Navel Chakra:** A pearlescent orange disc, interconnected with the top of the Sacral Chakra: Our connection back to the Universe.
    - **Palm Chakras:** White discs over the palms of the hands bring healing and creative energy.
4. Now, send any excess energy down the body to your feet. Imagine it going out of the feet and down to the Earth Star Chakra.

CHAPTER 11

Embracing Your Gifts

'All we ask right now is that you live in love and joy. This shouldn't be something to fear. It should be a celebration.'

– THE AKASHIC RECORDS

You Have a Purpose

Somewhere in the great expanse of time and space, the Universe whispered you into being. It shaped the stars, spun the Earth into her perfect dance with the Sun and Moon and wove countless lifetimes of love, loss and resilience through your ancestral line; just so you could arrive here, now.

You are not here by accident. You are here because the cosmos dreamed of giving you this space to learn. When your soul accepted the calling to experience life on Earth, it was all planned out; the direction your life would take, the Red Threads of learning and understanding you would undertake, even reading this book right now.

Your family, friendships, cultural background and the very places you have lived and visited were all chosen with care to support your unfolding path. Nothing was random. Everything was designed to guide you toward a life of joy. And because joy is your soul's ultimate goal, it would never ask you to walk a path you couldn't achieve.

But how do we begin to discover what that purpose truly is? How do we recognize and embrace the unique gifts we came here to share? Now that you have the understanding and tools you need to embody your destiny as a Lightworker, you can begin to realize your purpose. In this chapter, we will explore how to uncover your Soul Purpose and step into your gifts with clarity, confidence and trust.

YOUR INNER CHILD

If you are having trouble uncovering your soul desires, turn your eye to the past. What did you enjoy doing most as a child? What made you laugh, joke and play? We are our most authentic selves as children, before society's expectations and prejudices set in. I recommend reconnecting with your inner sense of childlike play, and incorporating more of this back into your adult life.

Embracing Your Purpose

'If we all did the things we are really capable of doing, we would literally astound ourselves.' – THOMAS A EDISON

Contrary to popular belief, your purpose extends far beyond your career or mundane life. What it will be depends entirely on the type of goals your soul has selected and whether those goals are best expressed as a career. We are not just our work as denoted by a singular label, such as 'teacher', 'doctor', 'banker' or 'driver'. We are so much more than a collection of labels, so the first step is to release any pre-conceived labels life has assigned to you.

Imagine a different world where you didn't have any obligations, fears or financial restrictions. What if you didn't worry about what others think? What would you do with your time? What would bring you joy? Remember, I don't mean what society has told you that you 'should' do, but what brings you true happiness. The answers that arise first indicate your true aspirations. Pursuing these passions is what will raise your vibration and bring you into a life of joyful, 5D living.

Soul Purpose Concepts

Our Soul Purpose is often one or a mix of these three things:

NATURAL GIFTS: Often a skill we develop at a young age, which we then continue into adulthood. Examples are:

- Playing a musical instrument
- Painting
- Horse riding
- Dancing
- Acting
- Singing
- Sailing
- Writing

HIDDEN GIFTS: These are the gifts others notice in us – qualities that come so naturally we might overlook them or assume everyone has them. Try asking people you trust what natural gifts they see in you. If their answers resonate with you and bring you joy, it's likely these gifts are part of your purpose.

Here are a few examples:

- Animals and children naturally gravitate towards you
- Being a nurturing figure
- Making people laugh
- Helping others feel heard
- Protecting the vulnerable
- Creating a calm, safe space
- Speaking clearly with impact
- Being seen as trustworthy
- Lifting people's spirits

LIFE LESSONS WE HAVE EXPERIENCED: Have you navigated significant life changes or learnings or helped someone else through something and now people seek your guidance and support when they're facing similar challenges? Examples of this might be:

- Health issues
- Pregnancy and parenthood
- Learning to drive
- Backpacking
- Changing careers
- Going vegan
- Training your new puppy

JOURNALLING TIME

It is a common misconception that our Soul Purpose is our job or career, but the truth is it's anything that brings us joy. We are now going to journal on what that could be for you. Then, for this Chapter's Activation, I'll help you to access the Akashic Records via the Akashic Records Library so that you can receive guidance on your Soul Purpose. Consider the following:

- What was an average day like for you before the age of 7? What were the highlights?
- Now, consider what an average day looked like at 17. Again, what were the highlights?
- If you had no limitations or fears, what would a dream year look like? What would you be doing? List the highlights of that year.
- Consider your current life situations. What areas do you hope to leave behind as you move towards your Soul Purpose?

CHARLOTTE – FOLLOWING THE RED THREAD TO SOUL PURPOSE

Charlotte is someone who can clearly picture every step and Red Thread moment that has directed her towards her light. From a young age, Charlotte was endlessly curious about how people think, feel and connect. That curiosity led her to study psychology at university, fascinated by the mind and its potential. What she once dismissed as a coincidence began to feel different as she deepened her awareness. Inspired by her university days, she often remembered the words of Carl Jung, '*There is no such thing as a coincidence.*' She went from curious observer to seeker, wondering what to do with the knowledge unravelling before her.

It took many years of personal work before she embraced her Lightwork profession. Along the way, every career choice, from psychology to corporate training, gave her skills she would later transfer into her spiritual work. She now sees that nothing she learned is wasted; every skill, challenge and detour is part of the map to our purpose.

Seeing the Red Thread

As her awakening unfolded, the dots began to join. Psychology blended with metaphysical teachings, spiritual philosophies and ancient energy practices. What began as separate fragments – ideas, studies and intuitive moments – now formed a coherent picture. Her intuition sharpened, synchronicities became undeniable and she could see how everything was woven together.

Teaching Others to See Their Own Red Thread

Today, through her business, Soulchak, Charlotte helps others recognize the same patterns in their own lives, guiding them to see their Red Thread. She teaches that your life is already telling the story of your Soul Purpose; you just need to learn how to read the thread and when you do, every step makes sense.

KEY TAKEAWAY: Your Soul Purpose is never random; every chapter of your life is part of the Red Thread guiding you exactly where you're meant to be.

Aligning Your Soul Purpose with Your Career

Now it's clear that your Soul Purpose isn't just your job, you might already know what it is and have embraced it in one way or another. Perhaps it could be a hobby or side hustle around your other roles.

However, if you want to turn your purpose into a career, how you achieve this is by aligning your job with your natural skill sets. For example, you might make a list of job roles – spokesperson, teacher, researcher, host, activist, creative, pioneer, caregiver – and then think about which one best suits how you could personally offer your light to the world? From there, consider whether you prefer online or in-person roles. Are you more suited to one-to-one or group interactions? If groups, how big are they? As you get more and more specific with your questions, you will land on a role that is most aligned with your soul gifts.

Telling Our Egos that Change is Coming

When you start to plan your dream future, your mind might come up with reasons why change isn't possible. Sometimes these points are valid and need to be overcome but most of the time it is the ego.

The ego knows that your current daily routines keep you safe, so its goal is to use negative thoughts to ensure you keep doing what is safe, but we know that isn't the purpose of our lives. When we need to step out of our comfort zone, these negative thoughts bubble up as a wave of reasons to resist change.

While we cannot always get past our ego's negative thoughts, we can realize it's not telling the truth. These days, I think of my ego with love, it's trying to protect me and for that, I am grateful.

So, when you fear what others think, you don't know where to start, or worry about having the time, skills, budget or a plan in place to make these changes, take a moment to thank your ego, breathe and bring in your intuition for guidance. Its calming energy will instantly make things feel lighter. Feedback on those feelings will bring peace and put you back on track.

Ask your intuition each day for *the next one action you need to take toward your goal,* then do that one thing. This helps keep the ego calm as it's not focusing on the bigger, more intimidating goal.

I have followed this process for years and witnessed it subtly taking me out of my shy, reserved shell to someone who does TV interviews and speaks on stage. My intuition didn't ask me to leap from one extreme to another; instead, everything built slowly and in ways that suited me. Even if your goals feel impossible now, or you cannot comprehend how you will pivot to this new life, your intuition knows!

How it Might Unravel

At the same time, I understand you want to know what the next few months and years will have in store. I can't predict what your intuition will suggest, but I've been through the process numerous times. Remember, you have more than one Soul Purpose, so I know how this plays out. It is usually one of these three paths:

1. A side hustle becomes your 'bliss'

At the beginning, when we choose to explore our purpose, that journey often has to unfold alongside the life we've already created. If your purpose isn't something you want to turn into a career, your intuition will help you discover how to weave this soul-aligned work into the life you already have. It might gently guide you to make small changes, allowing you to enjoy what brings you bliss more often.

For those who feel called to turn their light into a new career, our intuition often suggests we start this process as something we build alongside our existing work. As it grows, your intuition may encourage you to make gradual shifts in other areas of your life, helping you create space to focus more fully on this new path.

As someone who has built several businesses, my advice is this: Wait until your intuition says it's time to commit to your bliss full-time. When it does, ask it every question you can imagine so you have a plan in place to make the transition as simple as possible. Then, when the moment comes, take the leap and celebrate.

2. Starting with the leap

In some cases, we want to live our light immediately. If you can do that, excellent! I'd still check in with your intuition to see if that is the right thing to do. Often, our intuition initially guides us to go a little slower so that we have the chance to learn more about the different possibilities available to us. Reviewing each step before making the next step can result in a more successful outcome.

Fast change can also be harder on those around you. Your intuition will help you navigate this with compassion and understanding. Remember, when we make changes to be happier, it can be confronting to others who haven't considered that options like this are available to them.

3. Your dream comes to you

Once we change our vibration, we become a magnet for our dreams. Remember, the Universe wants us to realize our purpose. As soon as it knows we are receptive to guidance, it starts working with us. I've heard numerous stories of people attracting the ideal person or dream offer. Many people have a limiting belief that *life should be hard,* so we doubt those scenarios, but these moments exist in a 5D lifestyle.

Light Code Activation: Unlocking Your Soul's Plan

Up until now, this chapter has explored the theory behind what your purpose might be. Now we are going to journey into the Akashic Records (see page 15), to read the plan your soul made for this life. When accessing your Akashic Records to learn about your Soul Purpose, many imagine entering a library known as the *Hall of Records*. This works particularly well as it grounds the process of accessing the records in a familiar experience like going to the library.

Once we are there, the messages you receive will come from the pages but how you receive those messages will depend on your intuitive skills. You might do the visualization and then, as you pick up the book, emotions might surface, you might gain sensations in your body, feel drawn to look at something in the physical world or see a specific colour.

If the messages detract from the visualization, wait until all the messages have come, then take deep breaths, relax and try to recall the image of the book.

It's Time to Remember

It is essential that you are as relaxed as you can be, so please take more time than usual to reach that state.

Journey to the Hall of Records

1. Once relaxed, imagine your Merkabah (see page 36) surrounding your body for protection.
2. Then see an etheric cloak slowly falling from above, wrapping itself around you. This is the Cloak of Truth and Love. When in place, it ensures that it allows through only that kind of information.

Entering the Hall of Records

3. Visualize yourself walking through a large, grand building with a polished marble floor. Consider what it smells like – is the space hot or cold? Can you hear anything?

4. See yourself approaching the grand corridor. You walk down it to a large, towering antique door. This is the entrance to the Hall of Records.
5. Imagine opening the door.
6. Take some time to consider what the library looks like and feels like. What colours are there? Are you on your own? Is there anything unique or magical about it?

Find Your Akashic Records Book

7. Then, have the intention of looking for your book. Trust your intuition and let it guide you to its location.
8. When you have found it, pick it up and look at the cover. Notice its size, colour and any symbols or images on the front and back cover.
9. As you imagine holding it in both hands, I invite you to recall the question you wish to ask. As we have done before, ask a question on a slow inhale, then imagine opening the book on the page you need. On a slow exhale read or receive the information.

Here are my suggested questions:

- *What gifts do I have that are qualities of a Soul Purpose?*
- *How should I use them?*
- *Is this something I should be doing now? If yes, what is the first thing I should do to achieve this?*
- *What general guidance do I need to know now about my Soul Purpose?*

Take your time to read the text and observe any images or symbols that appear. Continue asking questions and selecting pages intuitively.

Leaving the Hall of Records

10. With gratitude, return your book to the shelf.
11. See yourself leaving the Hall, shutting the large doors behind you.
12. Visualize yourself walking back through the grand corridor, through the rooms and out of the building.
13. See the Cloak of Truth of Love lift off you. Remove your protections.
14. Become aware of your feet, toes and surroundings. Bring yourself back to the present moment. Stay there for a few moments before you move.

CHAPTER 12

Your Spirit Team

'You are not alone, separation only makes you feel that way! Before humans awaken, they can only see their human friends and family but you have friends in all dimensions.'

– THE AKASHIC RECORDS

It Takes a Village

One of the challenges of being a Lightworker is the feeling of not quite fitting in. While others seem perfectly at home in their surroundings, we feel as though we're standing on the edge, watching rather than fully joining in. Conversations skim the surface when our hearts long to dive deep, and there's an ache of not belonging, like we're speaking one language while the rest of the world uses another.

The good news is that those feelings of loneliness soften once we learn to connect with our Spirit Team. Regularly tuning into the unseen world brings a sense of companionship, guidance and support unlike anything we can find in the physical, 3D realm.

Your Spirit Team is usually made up of one or more light beings who have been selected to journey with you, either for a specific time frame or task, or for your entire life. Your Spirit team may include Spirit Guides, Angels, Ancestors and Spirit Animals. Some Lightworkers also build relationships with Deities, Ascended Masters, their Council of Twelve or even the Galactic Federation, though these connections are often a little less personal.

These beings are part of your soul's wider circle, and each carries wisdom and support tailored to your path. Many have incarnated with you before. For example, many Starseeds incarnating now will find Galactic beings on their Spirit Team, while Angelic Souls will naturally feel drawn to the Angelic Realm. As your vibration rises, it becomes easier for them to connect with you, and for you to recognize and welcome their presence, and the insights they have to offer.

Meet Your Spirit Team

Now we're going to explore the different members of your spiritual support team so you can recognize them when they show up and know the best ways to work with them as they guide and support you.

Ancestors

Our Ancestors are a vital layer of spiritual support, watching over us from the realms beyond. The close association we have towards those in our bloodline means they are often the first non-physical energy we want to connect to. Even in the non-physical realm, they are also the easiest energy to tap into because it is the one most closely connected to our body's frequency. At the same time, if you are trying to connect to those who have recently passed, grief can make it hard for us to maintain the right frequency to connect. If you feel that might be causing some problems, wait a while and then try again.

These members of our Spirit Team carry the wisdom of our lineage and often step forward to help heal generational patterns, offering protection and guidance rooted in our bloodline. Whether you knew them in this lifetime or not, their presence can be felt through traditions, memory and the subtle ways they pass on strength and resilience. By connecting with them, we not only honour our past but also bring healing to our family line, both backwards and forwards in time.

Spirit Guides

These are non-physical beings assigned to help you navigate your soul's journey. They can be members of your Soul Group or Pod who haven't currently incarnated. Unlike Angels, who serve humanity as a whole, Spirit Guides are chosen specifically for you. They can appear in literally any form: the figure of a human, a Galactic being, animals, plants, even mundane objects. Their role is not to make choices for you, but to gently nudge, protect and remind you of the bigger picture of your soul's path.

People often experience spirit guides as:

LIFELONG GUIDES: Always by your side, offering general support and protection.
SPECIALIST GUIDES: Stepping in when you need help with specific lessons or skills.
ANCESTRAL GUIDES: Family souls connected to your lineage who walk with you.
TEACHER GUIDES: Bringing wisdom from higher realms or past incarnations to help you grow.

Angels

Before connecting to the Angelic Realm, you need to understand the structure of the high frequency network of the Angelic Kingdom. There are numerous types of angels, from our Guardian Angel, who is with us throughout our life, watching over us, to the Archangels who have specific roles more associated with mankind in general than individual people. Most of the time, people ask the Archangels for guidance and support, but it is hard for them to respond to everybody's call, so they are not necessarily the best angels to support you. Please know that there is an Angel who specializes in literally anything you might need help with. Since these Angels are lesser known and not called on as regularly, they are more likely to be available, so you might want to try them first.

Types of Angels

GUARDIAN ANGELS: Will be assigned to protect and guide individuals throughout their lifetime.
ARCHANGELS: Leaders among angels, responsible for significant aspects of human life.
CHERUBIM: Keepers of divine wisdom and knowledge.
SERAPHIM: Are closest to Source and radiate pure love and light.
THRONES: Responsible for divine justice and authority.
VIRTUES: Bestow grace, miracles and blessings.
POWERS: Protect the world from negative energies and dark forces.
PRINCIPLES: Guide Leaders and organizations toward Divine Will.
DOMINIONS: Oversee angels and ensure Divine Order.

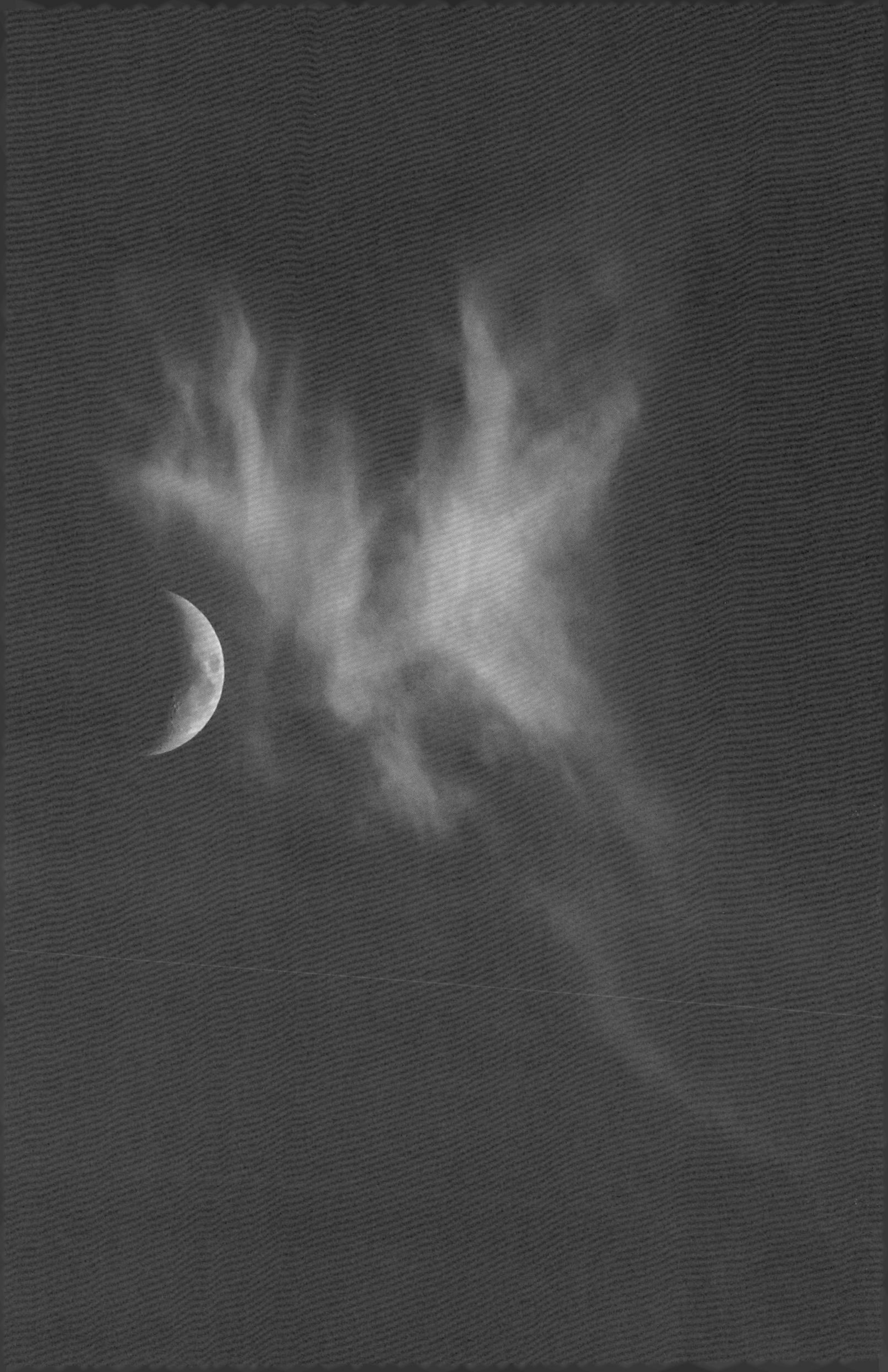

Spirit Animals

Animal Spirits embody the essence and medicine of the natural world. Each animal carries unique qualities, lessons and strengths. These guides can show themselves in physical form, if your intuition is drawn to an animal, even your own pet, and you think it might be a Spirit Animal, pay attention as the chances are, it is.

These allies remind us of our primal connection to nature and help awaken aspects of ourselves we may have forgotten. Unlike Spirit Guides who stay for long periods, Animal Spirits may come and go depending on the lessons and energy you need most in the moment.

Ascended Masters

Ascended Masters are highly evolved souls who once lived human lives and, through many lifetimes of learning, service and spiritual mastery, reached a state of enlightenment. They now exist on a higher plane of consciousness but continue to guide humanity. Because they have walked the Earth, they deeply understand the struggles and triumphs of human life. Masters such as Jesus, Buddha, Quan Yin and Saint Germain each hold specific qualities and teachings, supporting us in areas such as compassion, healing, forgiveness or transformation. When you call on them, you connect to timeless wisdom and a lineage of spiritual evolution that spans across cultures and faiths.

Deities (Gods and Goddesses)

Deities, also referred to as Gods and Goddesses, embody the archetypal forces of the Universe, representing aspects of creation, destruction, love, wisdom or protection. Found in every culture, they are honoured through ritual, prayer and offerings, something I have learned they do like us to do, not to bestow a hierarchy, but as a reminder that we should always have gratitude for those who help and support us.

Unlike Spirit Guides or Angels, Deities hold vast collective archetypal roles, which span all aspects of life, reminding us of the cycles of life, death, rebirth and the balance of cosmic forces. By working with them, we tap into the myth, story and sacred energy that has shaped human consciousness for millennia.

The Council of Twelve

The Council of Twelve is a collective of highly evolved beings who oversee the spiritual development of souls, and therefore also humanity and the Earth. They are often seen as wisdom-keepers, each one holding a specific ray of knowledge, truth or universal law. Together, they form a balanced circle of guidance, ensuring that cosmic order and Divine Will are upheld. Those who connect with the Council often receive profound teachings about collective evolution, soul contracts and humanity's role in the wider Universe.

The Galactic Federation

The Galactic Federation is an alliance of advanced star nations who work together for the protection and upliftment of Earth and her inhabitants. They are guardians of peace and unity, ensuring that the planet's spiritual evolution remains on track and is not interfered with by lower vibrational forces. Their members bring knowledge of healing, technology and higher consciousness, supporting humanity as it transitions into a 5D lifestyle and the expanded awareness and potential galactic reconnections it might offer.

Light Code Activation: Higher Heart Spirit Team Meeting

Now you have heard about your potential Spirit Team, it is time to meet them. We are going to connect to the Heart Chakra first, expanding its energy. Once expanded, our heart's energy can pick up on the energies of the Spirit Team.

This technique is successful for lots of people, but it is important you understand the process first before inviting in lots of energies all at once. For that reason, we are going to focus on bringing in just one of your Spirit Team. It might take a few attempts for you to align your energies but once you are there, you can have the intention that more Guides are invited to communicate as well.

How to Prepare

Remember, your Spirit Team is a much higher vibration than ours, so they have to work hard to reduce their energy in order to connect. Do your part and ensure you have done everything possible to be as high-vibe as you can before starting. This might include making sure you're hydrated, that you feel calm, have slept well, are eating high-vibration foods or regularly complete the daily Lightworker Lifestyle practices (see pages 163–7 and 172–3).

I would then consider bringing in lavender oil to heighten your intuition and a Labradorite crystal to help you pick up messages faster.

Connecting to Your Spirit Guides

Once you feel ready, move into a relaxing space where you won't be disturbed and follow these steps.

1. When you feel relaxed, visualize your Merkabah for protection and add the Cloak of Truth and Love (see pages 36 and 76).
2. Become aware of the area around your heart. Imagine a ring of pink light, close to the body.
3. Over a series of breaths, imagine that ring of light expanding more and more, until it reaches the walls of the space you are in.
4. Start to hold the intention that you would like to invite one of your Spirit Team to step into this circle.
5. When you feel ready, invite them to take one step inside.
6. Open up all of your senses and see if you pick up on any differences. For some, this will feel like a presence or a shift in emotions. Others might hear or see them or colours and sounds connected to them.
7. Then invite them to step out of the circle. Again, see if you can sense any shifts.
8. Now have them take two steps into the circle. Sense what changes that brings. Then have them step out again.
9. Finally, invite them to walk up to you. Consider how that feels. Then, on a slow inhale, start to ask them questions and see what intuitive answers come on the exhale. Here are some suggested questions:
   - *What kind of Guide are you?*
   - *Why are you visiting?*
   - *Do you have a message to give me?*
   - *Is this the best way to communicate with you?*
   - *How regularly can we communicate?*
   - *Are there other members of your Spirit Team who want to communicate with me?*
   - *Can you show me a sign that indicates you are near?*
10. Once you have finished asking questions, smile to raise your vibration more and show gratitude. At that point, you will see them leave the circle.
11. On the inhale, see that circle start to get smaller, stop when it's close to the heart again.
12. Remove your Merkabah and the Cloak of Truth and Love.
13. Open your eyes and ground your energies.

CHAPTER 13

The Lightworker's Lifestyle

'Many humans learn that big dramatic actions do not make the impact that small, regular, consistent actions can.'

– THE AKASHIC RECORDS

Maintaining the High

We've nearly reached the end, Lightworkers. You are so nearly there. By now, you have gained new intuitive insights, released heavy emotions and begun to connect with the deeper truth of your soul. You may already notice how much lighter, clearer and more vibrant life feels.

I remember reaching this stage myself and wondering: *Can it really stay this good?* The answer is yes. With the right daily practices, this higher vibration will become your new normal. Of course, growth never stops and life will still present its challenges that momentarily knock you off balance. But the key difference will be that you now have the tools to help you realign yourself more quickly.

In this chapter, I'll guide you through the foundations of a Lightworker's lifestyle. At its core is a morning routine designed to help maintain your higher vibrational frequency. These practices aren't just rituals; they're energetic anchors that help you remain steady no matter what life brings.

Your routine will weave together: gratitude practices, affirmations, journalling, energy boosts, aura cleansing, cord cutting and grounding techniques. Together, these form a toolkit you can return to again and again. Think of them as daily nourishment for your soul. The same way you would feed and care for your physical body, these practices sustain your energetic body. Ultimately, these lifestyle practices will allow you to move through the world as the Lightworker you came here to be.

Two Steps to Maintaining a High Vibration

To maintain a high vibration, start with being consciously aware of the areas of your life that lower your vibration and make changes where possible to reduce their impact. Then implement daily practices that will help sustain a higher vibration even during more complicated times.

1. Living Consciously

The key to maintaining a happier, higher vibration is to recognize the outside sources that bring us down, whether it be people, places, activities or things.

Take out your journal and brainstorm potential energy-draining situations. Then consider how you can improve each situation or how you see it. You can even ask your intuition what changes you should make.

2. Daily Rituals or Routines

Alongside step one, add at least one activity each day that can raise your vibration and increase your emotional and energetic resilience. It is worth doing these activities soon after you have woken up to avoid them being sidelined later in the day. This allows you to start the day on a higher-than-normal vibration, making it harder for stressful situations to affect you.

As long as they bring joy, the activities you pick are entirely up to you, but some classic suggestions are a good place to start. The best activities for overall wellbeing are good sleep, time in nature and meditation.

A LOVE OR HATE RELATIONSHIP WITH MEDITATION

Many people are resistant to meditation. Often, they don't like the idea of sitting in silence. In a world where we are constantly bombarded with information, moments of quiet are more needed than ever. Yet for many, the idea of trying to meditate feels uncomfortable, even overwhelming.

In reality, meditation is simply the act of focusing on a repetitive action. Therefore, if traditional meditation isn't for you, consider other repetitive activities that can offer the same calming, grounding effects, such as walking, running, breathwork, skipping or knitting.

Intuition, Intuition, Intuition

You already know that the best Lightworker skill we have is our intuition, so taking the time to connect to your intuition each day is always going to be valuable.

Each morning, I ask for guidance for the day ahead. Then, if I have the time, I also ask for insights on anything else that might be coming up. Sometimes the messages don't make sense at first, but I know that as things play out, the messages will become clear.

It is in moments of stress that we seek intuitive support. The problem is that in those moments, the body goes into survival mode, disconnecting us from our intuition. This is why I urge people to receive intuitive guidance each morning so they have already received guidance before they need it.

Three Lightworker Morning Routines

Alongside connecting to our intuition each day, gratitude, affirmations and journalling are the most valuable morning routines. Each one helps raise our vibration by changing how we see our current situation.

If you have the time to do all three each day, you are a spiritual rock star. If time restrictions mean you can only add one of these in with your intuition routine, then go for it! If you like variety, you might do a different one each day.

1. Gratitudes

The most difficult time of my life was when, after a bad relationship and several poor decisions, I found myself with only £72 in the bank – and I was homeless! I felt fearful about what I should do, and I was too ashamed to reach out to my family and friends for support.

In that moment, I realized that I needed to go back to the spiritual basics: gratitudes, affirmations and journalling. Gratitudes are about being grateful for the small things so that the big things can come. I practised being thankful for my sight, the fact I could speak, the nights I had a roof over my head and food to eat. I felt each gratitude deeply. As it lifted my spirits, I could feel it lifting my vibration.

That time taught me the true value and impact that these simple spiritual practices have and the changes they can ignite. Just over a year later, I had a job, could afford to rent somewhere and my now husband had come into my life.

WRITING GRATITUDES

Spend a few moments each day listing up to ten things you are genuinely grateful for. Try to list different things each time and as you write each one, see if you can experience the feelings of love and gratitude for each one.

2. Affirmations

An affirmation involves making a statement about something you want to bring into your life. For that reason, it is the perfect activity to do after the Quantum Manifesting Activation on page 116.

WRITING YOUR AFFIRMATIONS

Affirmations are short, positive, present-tense statements that focus on you, so you need to use words such as: I or I am. Examples might be:

- I am living my Soul Purpose.
- Every day I'm living in joy.
- I receive intuitive guidance daily.

Make sure you say your affirmation as often as possible. At first, the statement will feel uncomfortable. If you say a word quickly, slowly, mispronounce it or miss it altogether, consider this as the body struggling to form new neural connections to accept the new reality you are forming. This is normal, so keep going – you will get there.

3. Journalling

Feelings of stress, being overwhelmed or anxiety create a lot of negative energy in the head. Writing down what is concerning you clears the mind and its noisy mind-chatter. It is the perfect morning routine to implement when you feel things are becoming too much.

MORNING JOURNALLING

When you feel overwhelmed, journal each morning for at least seven days. Your target is to fill three A4 sheets of paper each time, which is enough paper for you to have written down all the obvious things that are on your mind. Once those thoughts are cleared, there will be a period when you struggle to write anything. Keep going because after that the underlying emotions or concerns come to the surface.

I have now run my businesses for over 14 years. At times, things have been stressful and I have had to make some tough decisions. In those moments, I always return to journalling. On those days, if I wake up with a stress level of maybe four out of ten (ten being high stress); journalling will reduce that score so I end the day at a five or six, rather than eight or nine.

START TOMORROW!

I invite you to start that daily routine right away. Try all the activities, then keep only the ones that bring you joy. Coming from joy is always the most important thing to consider!

Crystal Grids for High-Vibe Manifesting

While daily practices like gratitude, affirmations and journalling help you maintain a steady vibration, sometimes you will want to supercharge your intentions. That's where crystal grids come in. Unlike the smaller rituals that anchor you day to day, a grid acts like a long-term amplifier, broadcasting your desires into the Universe around the clock. Think of them as a higher-level tool in your Lightworker lifestyle, one that takes the intentions you set in your morning practice and magnifies them through the combined power of crystals and your focused intention.

I like to think of Crystal Grids as the original vision boards. Instead of images of things you wish to attract into your life, you're working with crystals whose energies align with what you wish to attract. The grid itself is arranged in shapes drawn from sacred geometry, which are patterns found both in nature and in the atomic structure of crystals. When you place your chosen crystals into these formations, you are aligning your goals with the very energies of the Universe.

The act of creating a grid also calls in the Law of Intention, focusing your energy as you decide exactly what you wish to manifest. Once activated, the grid continues to work with the Law of Attraction, drawing your aspirations toward you.

Most people build crystal grids as separate layouts in their home (see the image opposite), but as your vibration rises and you begin embodying 5D consciousness, the relationship shifts. Your energy becomes more crystalline in nature, meaning that you can begin to physically become a part of the grid yourself, integrating your body into its design. This is one reason why Lightworkers often talk about 'becoming crystalline' as you can learn to hold, sustain and channel higher frequencies, just like the crystals do.

What you will need

Source two crystals that represent what you want to bring into your life. Six small clear quartz points and one natural Citrine.

NATURAL CITRINE

This is the crystal of pure joy and happiness, so it helps us reach the high frequencies we are aiming for in this exercise. For that reason, I would carry this crystal with you, even after you have finished this exercise.

Manifesting with Human Crystal Grids

Start by placing your Citrine crystal out on the windowsill for a day to charge it with sunlight. This amplifies its energies even more. Sunshine also activates the Inner Sun, so try and do this exercise outside on a sunny day.

1. Find a spot where you can sit without being disturbed.
2. Place the six Clear Quartz points around you, facing towards you.
3. Place the two crystals by each hip.
4. Then hold your Citrine between your heart and solar plexus so we can connect your heart to your Inner Sun.
5. Say the relevant line: *I step into a life with . . . !*
6. Imagine a ball of yellow light coming out from your Citrine and surrounding you.
7. Stay there for five to ten minutes, then let it go back into the crystal.
8. Remove all the crystals and place them slightly away from your body.
9. Stay there for a few moments, ground your energies, then stand up.

Raising Your Vibration

Life happens and sometimes your vibration will deplete. You may find you need an extra boost to your frequency quickly. In those moments, the following tools and techniques are perfect.

Positivity Energy Blasts

This is a focused practice designed to elevate your mood and vibration by flooding your mind and heart with genuine appreciation and positive thoughts. It's like a turbo-charged gratitude session that lifts your energy and shifts your perspective. When you need a pick-me-up, do the following:

1. Find a quiet spot where you can sit with your notebook and pen.
2. Without stopping, write down everything you appreciate. Don't overthink it, just let the words flow freely and naturally. For example, you might write: *'I appreciate the sunshine, the sound of birds, my computer, my health, my creativity . . . '*. Make sure you feel gratitude and joy for each and every thing you write down.
3. Keep going until you feel a positive emotional shift.

Aura Cleansing

Our energy field can hold on to lots of unwanted excess energy that it picks up during the day. As this energy builds up, you might start to feel low without being able to pinpoint why. Clearing this build-up as often as you can is a straightforward way to keep your energies high.

Selenite wands are the perfect Aura Brushing tool. Here's how to use one:

1. Hold a Selenite wand about 5cm (2in) away from the body over the navel.
2. Holding the intention that the Selenite wand is removing any unwanted energy from the aura. Slowly move the wand up the body to the crown.
3. At that point, imagine there is white light to one side of you. Imagine that you flicked any unwanted energy into the white light.
4. Do this process again until you have brushed the wand over all areas of your upper body.

5. Then do the same for the lower body. Imagine you are brushing from the navel down to the feet. When you get to the feet, see yourself flicking unwanted energies into the white light again.

Cord Cutting

We all have a person in our lives who drains our energy. After spending time with them, we can feel physically and emotionally low. These people are often called Energy Vampires, which I feel is an unfair term, as it implies that they have deliberately taken our energies: most of the time it is an unconscious process.

When this happens, an energetic cord forms between us and the person draws on our energy. The same can happen when we enter a specific location or meet a particular group of people. In all these cases, the process of drawing away our energies is the same.

Cord Cutting with Black Obsidian Arrows

Humans have a long history of working with Black Obsidian. During the Stone Age, it was shaped into arrowheads. Today, we use these arrowheads and their cutting properties to cut through energetic cords.

HOW TO USE A BLACK OBSIDIAN ARROW

1. Close your eyes and take some deep breaths.
2. Think of the person, event or location that might have taken your energy.
3. Imagine an energetic line connecting you both.
4. Wave your arrow through that line, energetically cutting that cord.
5. Now, visualize your energy returning to you, the energy of the other person or place returning to them.
6. Imagine white light healing the cord and everyone involved.

Hint: One clue that a cord has been created is when we think of a specific person or play out a specific event in our minds again and again.

Grounding Our Energies

Finally, when we are stressed, a lot of energy collects in the mind, which we can experience as overwhelming or negative thoughts. When this happens, you can calm the energies by returning some of it into the ground. The fastest way to do this is to stand barefoot on grass and imagine the energies going back into the ground.

Alternatively, lie down with a Black Tourmaline crystal placed under your feet. Like a magnet, this crystal draws the unwanted energies out of the body.

Light Code Activation: Seeking Your 5D Lifestyle

As you become adept in Quantum Healing, I invite you to explore the idea that we can access the future now. That means we can communicate with the energies of our future selves to see what morning routines suit us the best. In this Activation, we will be asking 'future you' which daily rituals you should prioritize first.

Receiving Guidance from the Future You

1. Once you feel completely relaxed, imagine the future you walking towards you, sitting down in front of you. Consider what they look like.
2. To start the dialogue, ask them for *any general guidance they want to offer*. Remember to ask the question on a long, slow inhale, then open up your senses to receive the answer on an exhale.
3. Start asking them what your ideal daily routine should include. Here are some suggested questions:
   - *What activities suit you best?*
   - *Should you maintain those activities long term or will they change over time?*
   - *How long should you do them for?*
   - *What time of day should you do them?*
   - *Is there a different activity that you should include?*
4. Once you have finished asking all your questions, thank them and see them stand up and walk away.
5. After a few more moments, open your eyes.

CHAPTER 14

Your Double Mission

'Don't put pressure on yourself to change the world. You are already doing more than you realize.'

– THE AKASHIC RECORDS

Double Mission Lightworkers

Now that you have learned all about how to maintain your frequency, it is time to take your work to the next level. Some Lightworkers come into this life with not just one, but two missions. The first is a personal Soul Mission, which we have explored throughout this book. The second is a collective mission – a calling to assist in Earth's Ascension and the awakening of humanity. Many Double Mission souls are Starseeds or Advanced Beings who volunteered to incarnate now. They have come to support the shift from 3D to 5D consciousness and often feel this purpose deep in their being.

We will now learn what Double Missions are, how they unfold and how to recognize if you carry one. We will learn about the challenges and gifts that come with a Double Mission and look at the unique ways these souls are helping to shape Earth's transition into a higher state of being.

What Makes a Double Mission Lightworker Different?

These souls tend to awaken to their gifts at a young age, often triggered by intense life events. Their challenges push them into alignment with their Soul Purpose, creating space later for their second mission: global service. This might include:

- Teaching or healing
- Creating new 5D systems (in health, education, or governance)
- Holding space for collective grief
- Channelling higher wisdom
- Helping others remember their own soul paths

But remember – you don't need a title or fancy job description to fulfil this role. Often, just living consciously is the mission: quietly modelling a new way of being.

Night Missions

Some Double Missions can take place at the most unexpected times – even while you are asleep. If you wake up tired or feel like your dreams were intense or busy, your soul may have been acting out specific tasks such as sending healing or anchoring high-frequency codes into the Earth's grids. Some souls who can project healing energy or astral travel could be doing this work while they sleep.

WHAT ARE EARTH GRIDS?

Just like us, Earth has its own energy meridians, known as ley lines. Many of these lines are connected to sacred sites such as the Pyramids, Stonehenge and Uluru. Over time, the healing energies that run through these lines have been depleted after centuries of fear-based living. Double Mission souls help reactivate them by sending love, light and frequency into the grid. As these revitalized lines travel around the world, they carry those messages like echoes through the grid, encouraging the global collective to wake up.

Other examples of a Double Mission include:

- COLLECTIVE SOUL HEALING: Joining other Lightworkers on the astral plane to transmute trauma energy from past, present or future timelines.
- SENDING ENERGY TO KEY PLACES: Sending high-frequency healing to regions experiencing unrest, natural disasters or environmental imbalance.
- GUIDING OR AWAKENING SOULS: Helping others remember their soul origin or higher purpose while they sleep.
- TEACHING: Holding classes in the astral plane to help souls expand their awareness, progress their intuition and reach their goals.
- INTERDIMENSIONAL DIPLOMACY: Meeting with Galactic Councils in order to exchange wisdom, plan future events or assist with Ascension coordination.

Transmuting Pain

Over the years, as both a hypnotherapist and later as an Akashic Records Reader, I have learned that many Lightworkers have agreed to take on and transmute negative energies as part of their Double Mission. Some Lightworkers transmute the energies of individual people, while others take on the negative frequencies of locations, communities, whole countries or even Mother Earth herself.

Although their souls signed up to do this work before they incarnated, it can prove a lot harder on their physical bodies than they realize. If you experience ailments and pains in your body that cannot be explained, or you are an empath who takes on the emotions or physical ailments of those around you, learning to transmute the energy, using the Violet Flame (see page 125) is going to offer great support. Crystals such as Malachite can also help the body.

Self-Care for Double Mission Lightworkers

Your mission is sacred – but so is your rest. If you intuitively feel you are completing your Double Mission in your sleep, it is okay to ask for a night off. Simply set the intention for a restful sleep before bed. Overall, stay grounded and protect your energy with strong boundaries. Use your energetic tools and establish your daily energetic hygiene rituals. Seek regular guidance from your intuition and your Spirit Team.

IS THIS FOREVER?

Not necessarily. A soul's Double Mission does not always last a lifetime. Just like our personal missions, they often come to a natural end. Once a particular mission is complete, a new one may arise, or your focus may shift toward a quieter phase of anchoring peace, teaching or simply being.

STEVE – FROM 3D TO 5D AND LIVING HIS SOUL MISSION

When you meet Steve Nobel today, you find a man fully immersed in his soul's calling, running 'The Soul Matrix', a thriving platform supporting Energy Healers, Lightworkers and Starseeds through Ascension. With hundreds of thousands of subscribers, international events and a library of online content, Steve's work is deeply woven into his Soul Mission.

The Red Thread through Life's Challenges

Steve describes the spiritual path as one that often makes sense only in hindsight. Like many Starseeds, his incarnation into 3D reality brought challenges and relationships that clashed with his true nature. He calls this *dynamic tension,* the way people and circumstances can act as a springboard toward our awakening. Often, the soul begins in an environment opposite to where it's destined to go, so the contrast itself becomes the lesson. Looking back, Steve sees how each experience, no matter how difficult, prepared him for his calling.

A Shift in Perspective

I first met Steve when we worked together at an events organization where he was director for 13 years. Hosting some of the world's most prominent spiritual speakers, Steve felt he had heard it all but this was another lesson he needed to go through – the Universe is constantly expanding, as is our understanding of it. Now in his early sixties, he continues learning daily.

Lessons for the Awakening Path

- SURRENDER TO THE JOURNEY: There's no fixed endpoint. Your future self is always calling you forward.
- SEEK ACTIVATION IN SPIRITUAL PLACES: Sacred sites and like-minded company awaken deeper layers within.
- HOLD THE LIGHT: Don't wrestle with the dark – outshine it instead.
- KEEP IT LIGHT: Joy and playfulness are vital parts of the path.

KEY TAKEAWAY: Trust the process, embrace authenticity and seek high-vibrational spaces. The awakening path is rarely straight, but it always leads where you are meant to go.

Light Code Activation: Understanding Your Double Mission

In this deep visualization, I'm going to take you to the moment in between lives, when your soul picked your current Double Mission.

Remembering Your Double Mission Between Lives

1. Become aware of the Merkabah (see page 36) surrounding your body.
2. Make sure you focus on your breath as you feel your energy body joining the Merkabah. Then both of you start to float upwards gently, through the clouds, past the planets and further up into the stars.
3. Have the awareness that you are passing through dimensions and layers of light, arriving into a vast, peaceful realm – the space between lives.
4. Take a moment to look at yourself from this higher perspective. What do you look like in this state of pure energy? Can you still make out your features or are you a colour, sound, vibration?
5. In the distance, you sense the presence of wise, loving beings, your Council of Twelve. They are here to guide you on choosing your Soul Purpose. Listen to what they say.
6. Take a deep inhale, then on the exhale you see them ask you: *What do you want your Double Mission to be?* In your own time, see yourself state the answer.
7. Take a moment to ask yourself:
   - *How do you plan to complete this mission?*
   - *Is there any guidance you should know to make this process easier?*
8. As this moment comes to an end, allow yourself to receive a symbol that holds the frequency of your Double Mission. When you see this symbol in everyday life, it will remind you of your Double Mission.
9. It is now time to return inside your Merkabah. See yourself going past the stars, planets, through the clouds, to your room.
10. Once you know you have returned, gently bring your awareness back to your breath.

CONCLUSION

Living Your Light

'Be the magic you want to see in the world.'

– THE AKASHIC RECORDS

Last Word

As our journey together comes to an end, I hope you can now see your life through a very different lens. May you also see yourself as a soul first, who is wiser than we realize and has more experience than we can comprehend.

Perhaps one day you will look back and pinpoint *Find Your Light* as one of your Red Thread moments which helped direct you in the ways you needed at that time. May it have reconnected you to your soul, your intuition and your Spirit Team so you can live a life of true magic.

Remember each goal met is not an endpoint but part of a much bigger journey; instead of looking for that end, sit back and enjoy the ride. If a difficult moment comes in the future, the difference now is that you have the tools and understanding to support yourself and lift your energies. If you can remember to select an oracle card or tap into your intuition every day, in those more difficult moments you will already have the insights to see you through. You are empowered to ride the rollercoaster of life but this time you have the controls.

Lightworkers might feel different but wanting to live your purpose and live from authenticity should be normal. People are waking up to this so, although you are one of the first, one day authenticity will be *mainstream.*

I encourage you to go out in the world and find your tribe. You are not as alone as I know some of you will be feeling. Connect with like-minded seekers, either in-person or online, learn a Lightworker skill or join a sound-bath or breathwork class. Your world will open up even more.

Remember: consistency is key. Lasting success as a Lightworker comes from aligning your heart, mind and soul, using your tools as extensions of your energy. With regular practice and a strengthened sense of intuition and self-trust, you will shine brightly, fulfil your purpose and inspire transformation in yourself and the world.

I'm honoured to have spent this time with you, helping you to Find Your Light, offering you the truths behind why we are here and what the plan for our lives really is. I believe in you and everything you can achieve. Embrace life and the experiences your soul planned for you. Remember, bigger changes in the world come from the small steps we are collectively taking.

Now, embrace your purpose and let that inspire others to *find their light.*

Light Code Activation: Embracing Your Soul Mission

I want to finish by inviting you to enter into the energies of your Inner Sun, the higher aspect of our solar plexus (see pages 50–1). It empowers us to step into the best version of ourselves, free from any fears of what others might think, so we can fully embody everything we have travelled here to become. In that process, it allows us to release any guilt or shame attached to realizing our dreams.

Inner Sun Expansion

You need a notebook and pen, plus an item of gold jewellery, such as a necklace.

For this exercise, you need to be sitting outside in the morning sunlight. Position yourself so the sun shines on your back.

CONNECTING TO THE INNER SUN

1. Once you are relaxed, put both hands over the solar plexus. Where your hands are placed, imagine a yellow light.
2. Now imagine that yellow light is expanding with every breath until your whole body is yellow.
3. Become aware of the sunshine on your back and start to imagine the beams of light passing through your body. As they do, consider the idea that each ray of light holds codes of information.
4. Now imagine the same sunbeam focusing its energy and shining straight through your solar plexus and out in front of you.
   As it passes through your body, it clears and cleanses your solar plexus, while also waking up the Inner Sun, which is situated just in front of the solar plexus.
5. As you hold the intention that you fully embody the energies of the Inner Sun, reach for your gold necklace and, with intention, put it on. As you feel it rest in place, imagine your whole body turning gold.
6. Now say out loud or write down who you would be, without fear or shame.
7. When you are finished, imagine yourself standing up and leaving this space as a gold being.

ENERGY TOOL CATALOGUE

ALL CHAPTERS

Master Energy Tools

These tools are multi-purpose and can be used to support most areas of life in your energy work.

Crystal: Clear Quartz
Essential Oils: Frankincense and Lavender

CHAPTER 2

Soul Origin Reconnection

Starseeds:
Crystal: Astrophyllite
Essential Oil: Blue Lotus

Earthseeds:
Crystal: Moss Agate
Essential Oil: Vetiver

Angelic Souls:
Crystal: Angelite
Essential Oil: Grapefruit

Elementals:
Crystal: Spirit Quartz
Essential Oil: Lavender

Supporting the Awakening Process

Awakening:
Crystal: Vanadinite
Essential Oil: Lemon

Remembering:
Crystal: Merlinite
Essential Oil: Rosemary

CHAPTER 3

Supporting the Energy Body

Lifting the Veils:
Crystal: Golden Healer
Essential Oil: Patchouli

Reconnecting to Your Energy Body:
Crystal: Clear Quartz
Essential Oil: Tulsi (Holy Basil)

Supporting Specific Chakras:

- *Root Chakra*
  Crystal: Garnet
  Essential Oil: Vetiver
- *Sacral Chakra:*
  Crystal: Aragonite
  Essential Oil: Geranium
- *Solar Plexus Chakra:*
  Crystal: Yellow Calcite
  Essential Oil: Bergamot
- *Heart Chakra:*
  Crystal: Green Aventurine
  Essential Oil: Magnolia
- *Throat Chakra:*
  Crystal: Blue Lace Agate
  Essential Oil: Peppermint
- *Third Eye Chakra:*
  Crystal: Purple Fluorite
  Essential Oil: Clary Sage
- *Crown Chakra:*
  Crystal: Howlite
  Essential Oil: Myrrh

Higher Chakra Support

Earth Star Chakra:
Crystal: Chiastolite
Essential Oil: Copaiba

Navel Chakra:
Crystal: Stilbite
Essential Oil: Cinnamon

Hand Chakras:
Crystal: Apophyllite
Essential Oil: Lavender

Inner Sun:
Crystal: Gold
Essential Oil: Lemon

Higher Heart Chakra:
Crystal: Amazonite
Essential Oil: Rose

Akashic Records Chakra:
Crystal: Cavansite
Essential Oil: Fennel

Past Life Regression Chakras:
Crystal: Lapis Lazuli
Essential Oil: Basil

Causal Chakra:
Crystal: Libyan Desert Glass
Essential Oil: Melissa

Soul Star Chakra:
Crystal: Spirit Flower
Essential Oil: Frankincense

Stellar Gateway Chakra:
Crystal: Moldavite
Essential Oil: Celery Seed

CHAPTER 6

Overcoming Specific Emotions

Fears:
Crystal: Red Jasper
Essential Oil: Juniper Berry

Blocks:
Crystal: Herkimer Diamond
Essential Oil: Clove

Limiting Beliefs:
Crystal: Lepidolite
Essential Oil: Lavender

Understanding Mirrors:
Crystal: Sodalite
Essential Oil: Black Pepper

Resistance to Change:
Crystal: Bismuth
Essential Oil: Wild Orange

Lifting Karma:
Crystal: Faden Quartz
Essential Oil: Red Mandarin

Forgiveness:
Crystal: Watermelon Tourmaline
Essential Oil: Rose

CHAPTER 7

Supporting the Physical Body

Physical Healing:
Crystal: Amethyst
Essential Oil: Oregano

Pain in the Body:
Crystal: Malachite
Essential Oil: Birch

CHAPTER 9

Shadow Work Healing

Lifting Hidden Emotions:
Crystal: Unakite
Essential Oil: Yarrow

Healing Past Lives:
Crystal: Dogtooth Calcite
Essential Oil: Peppermint

Ancestral Trauma:
Crystal: Black Kyanite
Essential Oil: Helichrysum

CHAPTER 10

Connecting to Your Intuition

Intuition:
Crystal: Labradorite
Essential Oil: Lavender

Translating Intuitive Messages:
Crystal: Blue Kyanite
Essential Oil: Lavender

CHAPTER 12

Spirit Team Connection

Ancestors:
Crystal: Bloodstone
Essential Oil: Myrrh

Spirit Guides:
Crystal: Smoky Quartz
Essential Oil: Lavender

Angels
Crystal: Angelite
Essential Oil: Grapefruit

Spirit Animals:
Crystal: Green Tourmaline
Essential Oil: Madagascar Vanilla

Ascended Masters:
Crystal: Golden Healer
Essential Oil: Neroli

Deities:
Crystal: Goddess Stone
Essential Oil: Melissa

Council of Twelve:
Crystal: Atlantisite
Essential Oil: Frankincense

The Galactic Federation:
Crystal: Astrophyllite
Essential Oil: Blue Tansy

CHAPTER 13

Living a 5D Lifestyle

Energy Protection:
Crystal: Black Obsidian
Essential Oil: Clove

Grounding:
Crystal: Black Tourmaline
Essential Oil: Vetiver

Inspiring a Consistent Daily Routine:
Crystal: Period
Essential Oil: Lime

Creating a Healing Space:
Crystal: Scolecite
Essential Oil: Frankincense

Empath Support:
Crystal: Pink Amethyst
Essential Oil: Eucalyptus

Double Mission Support:
Crystal: Carnelian
Essential Oil: Copaiba

THE CRYSTALS

In order to help you source the crystals needed for the activities and Activations in this book, we have provided a visual of each one below.

AMAZONITE

AMETHYST

ANGELITE

APOPHYLLITE

ARAGONITE

ASTROPHYLLITE

ATLANTISITE

BISMUTH

BLACK KYANITE

BLACK OBSIDIAN

BLACK TOURMALINE

BLOODSTONE

BLUE KYANITE

BLUE LACE AGATE

CARNELIAN

CAVANSITE
CHIASTOLITE
CLEAR QUARTZ
DOGTOOTH CALCITE
FADEN QUARTZ
GARNET
GODDESS STONE
GOLD
GOLDEN HEALER
GREEN AVENTURINE
GREEN TOURMALINE
HERKIMER DIAMOND
HOWLITE
LABRADORITE
LAPIS LAZULI
LEPIDOLITE
LIBYAN DESERT GLASS
MALACHITE

MERLINITE
MOLDAVITE
MOSS AGATE
PERIDOT
PINK AMETHYST
PURPLE FLUORITE
RED JASPER
SCOLECITE
SMOKY QUARTZ
SODALITE
SPIRIT FLOWER
SPIRIT QUARTZ
STILBITE
UNAKITE
VANADINITE
WATERMELON TOURMALINE
YELLOW CALCITE

GLOSSARY OF LIGHTWORKER TERMS

AKASHIC RECORDS READER: The Spirit Guide you receive when your soul is created. This Guide helps you plan the lessons you want to experience in each lifetime and keeps the record of that plan (known as your Soul Blueprint or Akashic Records) when you incarnate. When you go to the Hall of Records (see page 150), it is the Book of your Soul Blueprint you are looking for to receive guidance.

ASCENSION: Raising your vibration to align with the Fifth Dimension.

COUNCIL OF TWELVE: Guides overseeing soul pods.

DIMENSION: A plane of existence for different beings (including humans), defined by its unique energy and perception of time or the level of awareness a being holds.

ENERGY MEDICINE: Holistic tools and healing methods that balance and support the energy body.

FREE WILL: The ability to make your own choices.

GALACTIC FEDERATION: Interdimensional beings overseeing activities in various galaxies, including ours.

HIGHER SELF: Your soul's energy and wisdom while you are in a physical body.

QUANTUM HEALING: Healing that considers the influence of different energies and dimensions.

SOUL FAMILY: Connected soul groups supporting each other's lessons.

SOUL GROUP: A group of souls learning and experiencing lessons together on Earth.

SOUL POD: A group of soul families.

THE UNIVERSE: *Find Your Light*'s term for God.

ACKNOWLEDGEMENTS

To write a book about awakening light is, in so many ways, to be held by those who embody it and I'm endlessly grateful to you all:

To Louisa, thank you for planting the seed for this book. Your belief in a guide created specifically for Lightworkers set this project alight. I love working with you.

To Leanne, who invited me to write my very first book and has been a guiding light through every one that followed – your steady encouragement, clarity and care have shaped my path more than you know.

To Jaz, the intuitive eye behind so many of the designs. Thank you for helping these teachings come alive on the page, again and again.

I remain profoundly grateful to the whole team at Octopus Publishing, who have reached out each time with such warmth and enthusiasm. I am blessed to return to such a gorgeous, talented group of people. It is an honour to bring another book into the world with you.

To Holly, Michelle and Sarah, dear friends and gifted photographers, thank you for working with us again.

To my husband, thank you for championing me in every corner of my life. You stand beside each project with unwavering encouragement and this time you even embraced the idea that our summer holiday would become a writing retreat. Your support is felt on every page.

To the case study contributors, thank you for sharing your personal stories with courage and vulnerability. Your experiences will guide, comfort and inspire others who will recognize their own journeys within your words.

And to the wider circle – students, community members, ceremony attendees, fellow teachers and the unseen spiritual supporters who walk with us – thank you.